The Light in the Life
of a
Psychic Surgeon

By sharing what I love,
I hope to inspire and open the hearts of others.

Paula Jackson

The information contained in this book recommends to always inform your health care professional before starting any alternative or additional therapies, treatments or when making any major changes in your diet or exercise programme.

Psychic Surgery is an alternative therapy to conventional medicine, and it compliments any medical condition, or medicine the patient may be taking. Every patient is asked to continue any medication they may be taking and is always recommended to consult with their health care professional for advice, diagnosis, and treatment. We are not permitted by Law to diagnose or to claim to 'cure' and there are no guarantees that this form of healing can work for everyone.

Previous publications by this author:
Journal of a Psychic Surgeon - Published October 2017 through Amazon.co.uk

ISBN- 9798723623743

Cover design and photography by Paula Jackson, author.

Sir Arthur Conan Doyle

I was beyond excited to learn that I had been gifted the opportunity to work spiritually with Sir Arthur Conan Doyle. To assist him as his channel, in the automatic writing of his chapters within this book. New channeled messages and a short story not previously seen are included within these pages. It was an honour to work alongside this very knowledgeable and spiritual gentleman.

*Sir Arthur Conan Doyle in 1914

*Kind written permission has been given to Paula Jackson from The Conan Doyle Family Estate, to use his image and his name Sir Arthur Conan Doyle in this publication.

Dedication

In deep gratitude to Spirit, to all of the Psychic Surgeons, the Angels, guides and helpers who, on a daily basis come forward to help, guide, and protect me on my wonderful spiritual path.

Please note: *Psychic Surgeon channeled messages are shown in italics.*

CONTENTS

1. Baker Street

"The Baker Street mystery is solved… sounds like the start of my next book!"

This might seem an odd introduction to begin my book, but the synchronicities presented to me back in July 2019 were coming at me so thick and fast that they could not be ignored.

As the channel and healer working with the Spirit Psychic Surgeons since 2011, I have found that over the years on many occasions the Psychic Surgeons have 'nudged' me to let me know when I have needed to take action. This is exactly what happened and how it all started.

It began on 5th July 2019, I had been out driving in my car when a song came on the radio that I hadn't heard in ages, Baker Street by Gerry Rafferty. Like a lot of people, I love the saxophone instrumental within the song, so much so, that I posted it on my social media page together with a YouTube video of the song and I wrote, "Heard this on the car radio today, Baker Street, just love that sax." (This is not something I would not normally do.) The post was liked many times and I thought no more about it until two days later when I wrote "Wow I've just heard the song Baker Street on the radio, again. That's the second time in a week! Still loving that sax." More synchronicities were to follow.

The very next day I was stopped in my tracks when I reached into the freezer for some bread rolls and looking at the packaging label it read… Baker Street! After picking my jaw up off the floor, I decided to take a photograph and post it onto my social media page to see if any of my spiritual friends had any ideas as to what was happening. I posted...

"What is going on? I just took some bread rolls out of the freezer, and just look at the label… Baker Street!" I had many replies to my question:
"Maybe you are taking the Psychic Surgeons to London?"
"A Sherlock Holmes connection?"
"There is definitely a message in there somewhere."
"Could there be a Dr Watson joining the Team?"
It certainly was a puzzle, and I didn't have to wait long for the next synchronicity to appear.

The very next morning whilst eating my breakfast the song Baker Street was played on the radio, it is a completely different radio station to the one I listen to in the car. I almost choked on my porridge. I just had to post the story of events on my social media page, and I posted the following: "Well, if you have been following my posts about the Baker Street synchronicities that seem to be happening to me at the moment, I can report that this morning, Baker Street was played on the radio…again! Different radio station than before, this is really incredible. There seems to be a link to Sherlock Holmes so let's see what happens next." Underneath my post I added in a photograph of the detective Sherlock Holmes smoking his pipe.

Straight away I received a reply from a lady, "You may have a connection to Sir Arthur Conan Doyle helping you, working through you, or joining your Team. He was also a Physician and a Spiritualist and wrote a number of spiritual books, he works with a number of Mediums too. Google him and take a look at his books. He was the President of the College of Psychic Studies in London."
I thanked her for her reply and immediately questioned this with the Psychic Surgeons and asked for their guidance.
I asked, "Dear Psychic Surgeons have you asked for Sir Arthur Conan Doyle to come forward and help me?" *"Yes, we have."*

I asked, "Would it be appropriate for you to bring him forward now for me to be introduced to him?" *"Yes."* And with that the Psychic Surgeons raised both my hands up into the air, as if reaching out for something or someone and brought forward into my hands the Spirit energy of Sir Arthur Conan Doyle. Unbelievable!

Apart from the Psychic Surgeons and the healing Angels in my hands to do the healing, I had, up to this point, not had any other Spirit energy in my hands, so I just didn't know what to expect.

His energy was different to the Psychic Surgeons, a very gentle energy, felt quite soft in my hands. Not having planned this connection, it had completely taken me by surprise. I had not had any time to prepare questions to ask Sir Arthur, if I had, maybe our initial connection might have flowed a little better than it did. I asked him, "Sir Arthur is this really you?" "Yes" was the reply. "Are you coming forward to help me on my spiritual path?" "Yes." At this point there was no mention of a book. I asked him "Would you be coming forward to work with the Psychic Surgeons?" "No." "But you have been asked to assist me?" "Yes." Feeling overwhelmed with what was happening, I apologised that I could not think of anything else to ask him. I thanked him for stepping forward and that I was looking forward to us connecting again in the future. I then felt his energy disappear from my hands and my hands fell down to my sides. I sat there in disbelief, how lucky was I to have Sir Arthur Conan Doyle coming forward to help me.

The mystery was solved! I was so excited, I just had to share this final outcome on my social media page and that afternoon I wrote the following: "I have today been connected to Sir Arthur Conan Doyle (author of Sherlock Holmes) he is going to be working with me, not as a Physician with the Psychic Surgeons, but to help and guide me on the next stage of my spiritual path.

What an honour to have such a knowledgeable gentleman come forward to help me. And yes, he was responsible for the continued playing on the radio of the song Baker Street. Amazing isn't it how Spirit get our attention." Underneath my post I added a handsome photograph of Sir Arthur Conan Doyle taken in 1914. Immediately on my social media page people commented:

"Well done I'm not surprised you have amazing integrity" –

"It's all too amazing!" –

"I can hardly wait to read his writings (through you)" -

A little while later I received this comment:

"He will help you to be more thorough with your writing. He wants to work through you as a Psychic Writer, he is very intense because he wants the best results. He will keep going until he produces the results he is happy with. He's asking that you trust him to write for you." I replied, "What a revelation and what an honour, I feel quite emotional. Yes, he was a prolific writer, and thank you so much for this explanation, I am very grateful." She replied: "When I looked at his picture I felt he was trying to communicate, so I had to pass this on to you. He is quite strict with his writing so you may be up late some nights writing. He is a perfectionist. He says it will be hard work, but if you are willing to put your trust in him, he will give you good results. He knows you want to improve your writing skills, so he has come in to help. He's showing me a journal for you to write in. He prefers handwriting to typing. He was a Spiritualist, and he visited many Mediums when he was alive." I replied "Thank you again, I am lost for words, although not for long by the sounds of it. Who would have thought it? I cannot believe he would come forward to help little old me, my mind is blown."

Other lovely comments received on social media were:

"I was only asking you yesterday when are you going to start writing your next book?" –

"How strange, I visited his grave yesterday at All saints Church, Minstead at the rear of the graveyard!" –

"Well Paula you are going up in the Spirit world of celebrities, congratulations my love your new book has got to be good with him working with you" –

"I'm sure your book will definitely be a best seller!" –

"Such an amazing gift to come through" –

"He was a famous Spiritualist too" –

"He has great understanding of illness and knows that Western medicine is missing the point a lot of the time, so glad he has made contact. He has insights to share about healing" –

"Looking forward to your new chapter, so excited for you" –

"Paula you are on such a fantastic journey and thank you for sharing your amazing experiences with us all" –

"This is superb can't wait to see what's next... you are very lucky Paula" -

I asked the Psychic Surgeons if I was to start writing my book yet, and they replied *"No, there is more for you to do before you begin writing your book."* And yet, I still kept hearing the Baker Street song on the radio, I wondered if it was the trigger to let me know that Sir Arthur wanted to connect with me?

When I next heard the Baker Street song on the radio I immediately connected to the Psychic Surgeons and asked, "Was it time to connect me to Sir Arthur Conan Doyle again?" *"Yes."*
How exciting, I sat and waited for the Psychic Surgeons to bring through into my hands the Spirit energy of Sir Arthur. After only a few seconds of waiting both my hands opened wide and I could feel his new energy in them.

My hands moved up towards and embraced the cheeks of my face. I said, "Hello is this Sir Arthur Conan Doyle?" "Yes." I thanked him for coming forward to connect with me and I wanted to confirm that he wished to write through me, "Yes." I asked, "Would you prefer to write with my right or my left hand?" "He indicated by moving my left hand with a wiggle that this hand was his preference. I told him that I had purchased an A4 journal pad in preparation for our connection and my left hand was lifted into the air and he stroked my face, as if he was pleased to hear this. I wanted him to know I was serious about our connection especially after all the trouble he had gone to, to get my attention.

I am used to carrying out automatic writing with the Psychic Surgeons and writing many pages with them, their writing style is large letters much larger than that of my own handwriting style, so I was interested to see how I would progress with Sir Arthur. I placed my pen in my left hand and waited for Sir Arthur to begin writing. My pen glided smoothly across the page, his energy in my left hand was gentle and did not hurt me in any way. His letters were neat and small keeping them within the lines of the lined journal pad we were using. The following dialogue is only some of the conversation that took place that day between Sir Arthur and myself. Through the automatic writing he wrote three pages of A4 conversation which I won't divulge completely, as there are different topics that will be covered later on in his chapters. This time I was ready and during our connection asked him questions that I had already prepared, to which he then replied.

"I am Sir Arthur we will work well together dear Paula. I am pleased to connect to you. Yes, today is an introduction day, I need to familiarise myself with how you write and how well you receive my words. You are doing fine. We will make a good team you and I."

"I am looking forward to imparting to you all that needs to be shared in your book. I have many experiences to share, and it will be very interesting to your readers of this book, which will be quite sizeable for us to write." I asked, "Will we cover Spiritualism?" "I am pleased you mentioned this as it was dear to my heart when I was on the earth plane. I would like the picture of me to be included, it is important as it will give credibility to your book." I said to Sir Arthur "I like to get things right" and he replied, "I do know this, I am also a perfectionist we will have no problem getting it right. We will have a routine, so the music prompt is not necessary to connect. The Psychic Surgeons asked me to help you my dear we are going to write an excellent book for you, and you needed my help to do so. They have planned this path of yours meticulously and I am honoured to be part of this journey with you. We will sign off now. Thank you for the connection today."
Sir Arthur.

Wow, that connection was just incredible, I still can't believe it, Sir Arthur Conan Doyle is going to help me, Paula Jackson to write my new book! To my shame I have to admit I have never read any of his work, although I have watched some Sherlock Holmes films. This is going to be so interesting; I really am so lucky.
Sir Arthur's chapters can be found further on in this book.

2. My Spiritual Path

When I was only twenty nine years of age my father, George died suddenly of a heart attack at home; he was just fifty six years old. As you can imagine it was an enormous shock to us all.

I learned that dad had passed away at a quarter to nine on that Friday evening and that the clock in the lounge had stopped ticking at that precise moment. But on every anniversary of his passing we would always notice that a clock in the house would stop at that exact same time, a quarter to nine. I was not a spiritual person during this early part of my life and thought it a bit spooky when things like this were mentioned. I didn't know that spirit could stop clocks like that.

Now, more than thirty years on, I am told by friends who can see spirit that my dad is often around me, which I find most comforting because with his sudden passing I was not able to say goodbye to him. As I started to meet different spiritual people, they would pick up on dad's energy around me, a friend who came to visit me at home said, "Do you know who is watching us from over by the television?" I replied "No" feeling a bit nervous that we were being watched. "It's your dad." Oh I thought how lovely of him to drop by.

In 2012 I attended a Mind, Body Spirit event that was situated in a massive field with marquees, stands and tents. I decided I was going to have a card reading. During the reading the Medium said to me, "I have your dad here, he's looking around and asking, "What are you doing in a place like this?" I'm laughing because I knew exactly what he meant, we were in the middle of a field, in a marquee, surrounded by spiritual people. Our family were from the East End of London, we were not spiritual people and certainly would not have attended an event of this kind. But dad was in spirit now, so surely, he would understand why I was there.

The message he gave me during the reading confirmed that he understood the new path I was on, and that he was so proud of me helping so many people with the healing.

In 2017 I wrote and published my first book, Journal of a Psychic Surgeon and had a book signing day arranged very soon after it was launched to promote my book. Just before we were about to open the doors, my friend said to me "Who is George?" I replied, "George is my dad." I could feel the tears welling up in my eyes, I knew exactly why he was there with me, I knew he was so proud of me, his daughter having written a book, published it herself, and now I was doing a booking signing day. I knew he was watching down over me, to be there for me. My friend had sensed his presence which made me cry even more.

Spiritual contact with my dad was not a regular occurrence, but in October 2019 the most amazing connection between us happened. This particular day my car had broken down, I wasn't stranded but was waiting for the recovery service to collect my car and take it to the garage.

As the time passed my friend suddenly said, "I can feel your dad George is around you." I knew straight away that he would be concerned that I was having car trouble, maybe that was why he was there. Then my friend said, "He is showing me wholesome foods, he wants you to eat more wholesome food." I thought that was a lovely message to receive, but not very relevant to what was happening that day. If only I could hear him for myself.

Then suddenly a thought came to my mind, if I were to connect to the Psychic Surgeons and ask them about my dad maybe they could help me. I asked the Psychic Surgeons to come forward and they connected through into my hands.

In my mind I asked them "Was my dad around me today? *"Yes."* Then I asked them, "With their energy would they be able bring my dad to me?" *"Yes."*

I then asked the Psychic Surgeons, "Would you be able to bring my dad to me into my own hands now, just like I do with you?" *"Yes."* My heart was thumping in my chest, I wondered just what had I asked of the Psychic Surgeons.

Using their own immense energy the Psychic Surgeons raised my hands up into the air. My friend who was standing just a few feet away from me was wondering what was happening, I quickly said to her, "Watch this." My hands reached out into the air as if they were enclosing around something or someone. My hands were then brought towards my face, the palms of my hands pointing towards me. In my mind I asked, "Dad is that you?" And with that my hands (now filled with his energy) embraced my face and touched my cheeks and patted them over and over and over again. My dad was in my hands! It was the most beautiful, tender moment ever. Tears were streaming down my cheeks and my friend had tears too, she said, "I can feel his love for you, he really loves you". In my mind I said to him, "Dad I can't believe you are here I love you so much, I've missed you so much." My own hands with his energy in them, continued to pat my face over and over again. I asked, "Dad are you here today watching over me because the car has broken down?" "Yes." "Am I safe?" "Yes." "Am I going to get home safely?" "Yes." "Dad, do you have a message for me?" My friend then said, "He loves you and he is so proud of you." I thanked him for his message by bringing my own hands to my face and giving little kisses, hoping that he would be able to feel them. I then asked him, "Dad would you be able to make this connection with me again by yourself?" "No." "Can you only come to me if the Psychic Surgeons bring you to me with their energy?" "Yes."

19

So now I understood, the Psychic Surgeons immense energy had carried my dad forward in spirit to bring him into my hands so that we could make this beautiful Father-daughter connection. I asked, "Dad can you stay any longer?" "No." It was time to go.

I said my goodbyes to him in my mind and promised that we would do this again. My hands patted my face again over and over, the tears were streaming down my cheeks as I felt his energy leave my hands. And now he was gone. I then felt the Psychic Surgeons energy return into my hands, and I thanked them so so much for doing this wonderful thing for me. It was one of the most special moments of my life. I looked over at my friend and she was in tears just as I was, we gave each other a hug as we marvelled at this incredible happening, wondering did this really just happen? Yes, it really did!

Psychic Art

I had been talking with a new friend about psychic art and the wonderful drawings or paintings that these talented Artists do of peoples guides, pets, and loved ones who have passed to spirit. My friend suddenly said to me "You could do that you know, I'm sure you are meant to draw a portrait of one of your Psychic Surgeons." I have to admit I do love drawing and when I was younger was more prolific in my sketches than I had been of late. I decided to get my sketch pad out and to practice so I started copying a Christmas card with the beautiful image of a stag.

My charcoal pencil just flowed over the page; the image of this beautiful creature was suddenly starting to appear on my sketch pad. His antlers were a challenge though and had to be repositioned a couple of times on the paper. But the eyes and nose looked exactly as they should. I was encouraged to continue until the drawing was finished. I even captured the small bird on the shoulder of the stag as in the original image.

20

I was really pleased, this spurred me on to do another drawing. The next image I chose to draw was a rose, one of my most favourite flowers ever, so intricate with its many petals all folding into one another.

I drew a rough outline of the flower and added in some leaves, I then began to add more defined detail. I was so engrossed with the drawing the time just flew by. With my finger-tips I smudged the charcoal on the page to obtain a shadow and depth to the petals and again the image was exactly like the original.

Once I had finished drawing the rose, I chose other subjects to draw, a lady with a hat, a Ballet dancer, a Phoenix rising. I now wondered if it was time to ask the Psychic Surgeons if they wanted me to draw one of the Surgeons from the Team. I asked to connect to the Psychic Surgeons for them to step forward through into my hands and told them I had been doing some drawing and I wondered, "Would you like me to do a drawing of one of the Psychic Surgeons from the Team?" *"Yes"* was their reply. Oh how exciting! May I ask, "How are we going to do this? Do you have someone who could come forward into my hands to do the drawing?" *"Yes."*

Excitedly I got my sketch pad and the different types of pencils that I have, so that they were readily to hand. I asked the Psychic Surgeons "Would you please bring forward into my hands the Psychic Surgeon artist who is going to assist me in drawing their image?" *"Yes."* With that, the energy in my hands changed. I asked, "Are you going to help me draw a portrait?" *"Yes."* I picked up the charcoal pencil and just relaxed my hand over the sketch pad and suddenly my hand started to move! The pencil moved and drew a large oval in the centre of the page, and we had an outline of a face.

Next to be drawn was the hair, this seemed very important as many times my hand went over and over to get the strokes right for the hairstyle being drawn and there was lots of hair, quite a full hairstyle was emerging. My hand was moved away from the sketch pad and reached out to where the coloured pencils lay, I asked, "Do you need a coloured pencil?" *"Yes."*

I picked up the pack of pencils and my hand hovered over all the coloured pencils until a brown pencil was chosen. My hand was then returned to the page and started to colour in the hair, how amazing was this? These were not my hand movements; my hand was being moved to enable the spirit Psychic Surgeon artist to draw his own portrait. We continued to move down the face to his eyes, with slight bags underneath and wrinkles to show his age, then full eyebrows were drawn above them with tiny pencil strokes for each eyebrow hair. The attention to detail was wonderful to watch, because that was exactly all I was doing, watching, all of this was unfolding in front of my eyes! We needed another coloured pencil, and this time blue was selected, he had blue eyes. Next was his nose and great detail in the pencil strokes was used to ensure the roundness of the tip of his nose and nostrils. The mouth seemed to prove to be more of a problem, at first it seemed too small for the size of the features that had been drawn. My hand went over and over the mouth trying to get the proportions right. In the end I asked, "Should I rub out this mouth so we can start again?" *"Yes."* I took the eraser and removed the mouth image so we could begin again. This time he captured the size and shape of the mouth perfectly even shading around the mouth to show some beard growth and shadow. My hand was then moved up the page, I hadn't realised that he had no ears. The outline of ears was added first on the right side of his face and then to the left side. Once he was happy with this, lots of scribbling and circles started to be drawn with the pencil, what could he be doing?

Then it dawned on me he was drawing in sideburns in front of his ears! Looking at his image it looked to me as if this Psychic Surgeon was from the 1970's. I could be wrong, but it would explain the heavy hairstyle. We shaded his face all around the cheeks and jawline down to the chin. The neck and shoulders were drawn quite quickly but more time was taken as we started to draw the neckline of his shirt and then his striped tie.

Again my hand reached out to the coloured pencils and scanned across the coloured pencils available. I had a feeling that the colour he wanted was not there, so I asked, "Do you need a cream coloured pencil?" *"Yes."* Unfortunately, there wasn't that colour to choose from, so I suggested using the pale yellow pencil instead. This seemed to be acceptable, he then started colouring in the shirt collar and then with big bold strokes of the pencil he coloured in his shirt from the shoulders downwards. Then my middle finger was raised and started to rub the page to smudge the yellow pencil strokes to shade in the shirt. (How clever.) Next was his tie, I asked, "Is there a colour to your tie?" *"Yes."* I offered the coloured pencils, and my hand scanned the pencils until the green charcoal pencil was selected. It didn't take long to finish his tie and I asked him, "Have we finished now?" *"Yes."* I thanked him so much for coming forward to draw his portrait today and said it was lovely to see his image. The finished portrait can be seen as number 6 of the Psychic Surgeons images.

This has been an amazing connection and certainly one I never expected. The Psychic Surgeons use my hands so gently, whether it is for their wonderful healing or now as a channel for the psychic art. I wonder now what else they have instore for me?

3. Healing for Paula

I am so very lucky as an individual to be able to say that I am in excellent health, mentally, emotionally, physically, and spiritually. As the channel for the Psychic Surgeons I need to be 'tip top' in my wellness to provide them with the clear channel they need for their Psychic Surgeon healing. On a daily basis the Psychic Surgeons connect to me and if ever needed, give healing to me. After being with me for ten years now, they know me inside out, literally!

Just as they do for the patients, they scan me to find any areas that may be blocked or out of balance and apply their healing energy to me through my own hands. There is a surge of strong energy that I feel from them as they do their healing. It travels through my mind, body and soul. I am at times, physically moved around just like a little puppet on a string being moved about, as they access areas of my body that need their direct contact, which is then applied through my own 'hot' hands.

I wanted to share with you some of my own personal experiences of the Psychic Surgeons healing that has taken place on me, their channel. I know how the healing feels. The sensations felt are incredible and the description of 'wonderful' does not seem to do it justice. The feelings of unconditional love from them fill me from head to toe so that I feel loved and supported and my heart just wants to burst with love. I know how immediate the relief can be, when I have been in discomfort and it has been removed completely. I know how long lasting the healing is when my condition has been completely healed. The healing from the Psychic Surgeons is beyond words, I use the word 'amazing' a lot because you cannot find enough words to describe what you have experienced, seen or felt during a healing session with them.

My first cry for help was one Saturday evening in early October last year. I returned home from an all-day healing event that I had attended offering the Psychic Surgeons healing. The venue had been a couple of hours away by car and I had had a nice easy journey home, totally unaware that anything was wrong. But as I got out of the car the pain that shot down my left leg was like nothing I had experienced before, it was excruciating. I could not walk! My mind raced, what had I done? I had been seated quite comfortably driving the car and felt no undue discomfort during my journey.

But here I was standing beside my car unable to walk. I gathered my bag and I literally had to limp across the car park in agony. All I wanted to do was get indoors and see what I had done. The only trouble was, there was a flight of stairs to climb first to take me to my front door.

As I stood at the bottom of the staircase, I looked up at all the steps ahead of me. The way I felt, I might as well have been trying to climb a mountain! I gingerly tried to lift my left leg to place my foot onto the stair tread, I couldn't, because the shooting pains down my leg were excruciating, so much so that I cried out in pain. I had to rethink how was I going to get up these stairs. I decided to take one step at a time with my right foot leading to get up each stair tread. As I slowly ascended one step at a time, in my mind I was thinking what have I done?

I got to my front door and in my mind was already asking the Psychic Surgeons please come forward I need your help for some urgent healing please. I slipped off my coat and shoes and made my way slowly to my bedroom. I lay down on my bed and called for the Psychic Surgeons to come forward into my hands explaining in my mind to them that I didn't know what I had done but that I was in agony.

The Psychic Surgeons arrived in my hands, they scanned me with my own hands, stopping and hovering my hands above and over my lower back and legs. They worked quickly through my hands to apply the healing to relieve the pain and readjust whatever it was that had been misaligned. After about half an hour the Psychic Surgeons had finished. I thanked them so much for helping me.

I waited for a while to rest and absorb the healing energy. I then went to get up off the bed, and I could not. There was no power in my left leg to lift me, it felt like it was numb. The Psychic Surgeons do use anaesthetic during their surgery, and I guessed that they had done this to me, so using both my hands I hauled myself up using the foot post of the bed to enable me to stand and steady myself.

Then it suddenly dawned on me, I had a healing event in Wales the next day that I was booked into, and in my mind I thought, am I going to be well enough to attend? At this rate, the answer was definitely no!

All that evening it didn't matter where I put myself, I could not get comfortable, the pain was returning and shot down the outside of my left leg and was like nothing I had experienced before. So before going to bed at an earlier time than I usual would, I asked the Psychic Surgeons (I was pushing my luck here) if it would be appropriate to receive further healing from them? Usually the answer is *"No,"* as the healing has to be given time to do its work, but this time they said *"Yes,"* and I was so relieved to receive their lovely caring healing energy again.

I probably spent most of the night awake, it didn't matter if I laid on my right-hand side or my left the pain shooting down my leg was unbearable. I tried laying on my back, but that relief was only short-lived.

By 4am I decided I needed to visit the bathroom, and this would be a good test to see if the pain had gone away, well in one word NO it had not. I struggled as I had before to get to and from the bathroom and was limping badly.

As I returned to my bed I asked to connect to the Psychic Surgeons "Please can you guide me, do you wish for me to attend the Mind, Body Spirit fayre tomorrow?" *"Yes."* I asked them again if it was appropriate please may I receive more healing? *"Yes."* After about half an hour of physical healing and literally moving me around in my bed, the Psychic Surgeons were lifting each hip off the bed, one at a time and rolling me onto my side. Then turning me over so I could turn over onto my tummy, so they had direct access to my lower back. The feeling of their healing was so gentle, given that I was in a lot of pain, they just lifted it away. When the Psychic Surgeons had finished giving me their healing, I went straight off to sleep.

The next morning the alarm woke me at 7am. If I was going to attend the Mind, Body Spirit fayre, I knew I had to get up straight away and test to see if I could get out of bed. I swung both my legs over the side of the bed and placed my feet on the floor and with all my might pushed down on my legs to stand up, and I did it, I stood up with no pain! No pain whatsoever!
I was ecstatic. How fantastic are the Psychic Surgeons? I was pain free, the relief I felt made me emotional, I cried, I was so grateful to them all. I gently lifted my left leg and moved it without so much as a twinge of pain.

I was able to go about my business of the day, which was to get ready, and drive to Wales. In the car I wondered if my driving position would aggravate my left leg, but no, I was fine when I reached my destination.

I set up my treatment table and banner and with a fully booked day offered the Psychic Surgeons healing to others. No one knew or guessed the agony I had been in the night before. I did very well but by the end of the day I was starting to feel tired. I still do not know what set it off that day, but it was a trapped sciatic nerve. All I know is I never want to experience that pain again. The Psychic Surgeons came to my rescue, I said to them over and over, "Thank you, thank you, thank you, Psychic Surgeons you are amazing!"

Unbelievably in the same month of October I had another experience of needing the Psychic Surgeons healing. I woke up on a dull rainy morning to find I had slept heavily on my left shoulder and it felt quite stiff and achy. With my morning routine of connecting to the Psychic Surgeons I asked them to scan me please to see what I had done to my shoulder. Straight away they started giving me healing all down my left collar bone then to the shoulder ball joint, then down my left arm to my left hand. Even the underside of my arm felt tender. I thanked them for the healing and went about my day. But as the day wore on, my shoulder felt more and more uncomfortable to the point where I had to think twice before picking anything up. I went to bed around midnight and when I awoke the next morning the pain in my shoulder had increased. No longer just a niggle it was full blown 'pain' with very limited mobility in my left arm. What on earth is happening I thought? This is so unusual for me to feel so unwell and as you can tell, I'm not a very good patient.

That morning when I linked in with the Psychic Surgeons, I asked them "If it was appropriate to receive some healing today please?" *"Yes."* In my mind I was thinking thank goodness.
The Psychic Surgeons were in my hands and moved them and placed them over and above my left shoulder. The heat that was coming from the palms of my hands was immense as they gave healing to me from over my left shoulder and down my left arm.

This time I could feel them working inside my arm on my tendons, (a strange feeling) as apparently I had done some damage to them. As the Psychic Surgeons manipulated my arm raising it in the air, the pain was really at an uncomfortable level and I am such a wimp, that when it became too much to bear, it made me call out in pain. The Psychic Surgeons continued to work to correct the damage. As the pain continued, I asked them if they could anaesthetise my arm so that they could continue and remove my discomfort. Amazingly within seconds the pain and discomfort was gone. The Psychic Surgeons continued with the healing until their work was complete.

We had a full day ahead of us of distant healing appointments that had been booked. Throughout the morning the Psychic Surgeons were so considerate and kind. The anaesthetic was obviously wearing off and they could sense I was struggling to move my left arm, because at times my arm mobility was so limited that I could hardly raise it without wincing to complete the necessary movements they needed for their distant healing.

The Psychic Surgeons are able to take the physical weight of my own arm/s and make them feel as light as a feather and they had done this before for me. On this day they helped me by doing just that so I could move my left arm in order for us to complete the distant healing. They are just so clever, and I was so grateful. At one stage during the morning I asked them, "Was my limited mobility detrimental to the distant healing being given?" *"No."*

Once the mornings distant healing sessions had finished I sat down at lunchtime on the settee and relaxed. After eating my lunch the Psychic Surgeons were still around me and through my hands they came forward and gave me some more healing, without me even having to ask. They could sense I was in some discomfort and their healing was just so amazing it helped me immediately. And we continued with the distant healing appointments for the rest of the afternoon.

Each time my left arm or left hand needed to be raised, the Psychic Surgeons literally took hold of my left arm with my own right hand, and they assisted me and moved my left arm into the required position. I had never ever seen or experienced this with them ever before! I can honestly say that as the afternoon wore on, my left shoulder and left arm got easier and easier to move to the point that, by the end of the day I had no pain whatsoever in my shoulder or arm.

The Psychic Surgeons are so kind to me, so caring, we have a wonderful connection, and this is one of the reasons why I have written about my own health and wellbeing. Because I wanted to share with you just how caring they are towards me, their channel. I wanted to share what I have personally experienced during a healing session, and hopefully in much more detail than you knew before.

They were truly incredible healings that I received from the Psychic Surgeons, I asked so much of them and they delivered. They are so clever, and they are capable of achieving so much more. These are only a few examples of what they can do. But I'm certainly a good subject for them to practice on that's for sure. (She laughs).

4. Successes

Our first book
With more than 68 five star reviews on Amazon worldwide I can't tell you how thrilled I am at the success of our first book, Journal of a Psychic Surgeon. To be so well received has personally given me a tremendous boost. But more was yet to be revealed about the book itself, when readers of the book kept reporting how they 'felt' the energy of the Psychic Surgeons emanating from its pages and that they were receiving healing. How could that be? I needed to ask the Psychic Surgeons for their guidance and informed the Surgeons that people were reporting they were receiving their Psychic Surgeon healing when reading our book.

Their reply was, *"Yes my dear that is correct, you cannot be everywhere, but we can."*

I was completely shocked! The Psychic Surgeons were using our book to give their healing to anyone who was in need. It completely blew my mind. They are so clever. Our book was to be the first 'physical' tool the Psychic Surgeons were using to spread their healing around the world.

I began sharing this revelation to let people know that they weren't just purchasing the book for a good read, but that they would be receiving healing too. Even after three years since its publication our book is still being sold through Amazon. The Psychic Surgeons have guided me that this book too will also contain their healing energy. So if you turn to the pages containing the Psychic Surgeons images and place the open book over your heart chakra you will receive their beautiful healing.

Taking notes

After many years of working with the Psychic Surgeons, they informed me that they wished for me to start recording details from our healing sessions with the different patient's health conditions. They did not require me to do this with everyone that came for healing, but the Psychic Surgeons would indicate to me who they wished me to take notes on and with the patient's permission record the outcome of the treatment. The Surgeons aim was to enable people to read the case studies success and understand exactly what the Psychic Surgeons were able to achieve during a healing session and beyond.

* Name changed to protect the privacy of this person.

Scoliosis

*Penelope wrote to me to say "I am also a healer and a channel, and the Healing Ones who work through me did some work on my back and my back has healed to about 30%. I asked my spirit guides if my back would be completely healed, and I was advised to seek out another Psychic Surgeon healer to work on me. I don't know why, but I followed the instructions. I did a search on You Tube on psychic surgery and found you! Penelope asked if we could schedule a distance healing for psychic surgery on her back, her hip and the back of her neck. She continued, "I have scoliosis (a sideways curvature of the spine) which was only healed about 30% about two years ago with psychic surgery." We arranged a distant healing session of thirty minutes for Penelope, taking into consideration the time difference between our two countries as she lived abroad. I called the Psychic Surgeons forward into my hands and greeted them as I do each day. With the Surgeon's now in my hands we were ready to begin.

I gave them an overview of the lady's condition and before the healing started the Psychic Surgeons were scanning her body to establish her condition. The healing began and we used the full length photograph of Penelope which was needed for the Psychic Surgeons to make their connection to her.

As the distant healing started my hands were moved by the Psychic Surgeons over her photograph, first of all working around her head, reaching in and pulling out mental blockages that needed releasing, seen as black strands. Then moving to her heart chakra, releasing suppressed emotions that were stopping her body from healing itself. My hands were then moved up and down the length of her torso and I knew the Psychic Surgeons were giving healing to her back, as in her photograph she was front facing. My hands were then moved by the Psychic Surgeons to her abdomen then upwards to her stomach, which meant we were removing blocked energy from the digestive system. The Psychic Surgeons continued to clear and cleanse her Aura, to rebalance her chakras and finally at the end of the distant healing session completely enclosed her with pale pink unconditional love.

I then emailed Penelope with feedback of her distant healing session with my findings, and this was her reply.
"I'm very grateful for the work you do. I appreciate the detailed explanation. Thank you for clearing the blockages and suppressed emotions. I have suffered digestive problems so thank you for that also. I feel light and clear. The shape of my back isn't a pronounced S and has straightened out quite a bit with the distant healings. I am so grateful to you and the Team. She then wrote to me to say, Thank you very much for the second distant healing. I can tell by looking at my back that my spine has significantly straightened! Amazingly my back is now 60% healed!"

After the final distant healing had been sent to Penelope her reply was amazing to read. "Thank you Paula I am most grateful for all of the healings. 80% max healing for my back at this time aligns with my journey. Miraculous results!"

Wales

"I met Paula in Pembrokeshire at a Mind, Body Spirit show in October 2019, and I am so glad I did. Having had three wonderful children I had a condition that is known as Diastasis Recti, this is when the stomach muscles separate. I was no longer able to enjoy things I loved doing like running, swimming, and especially picking up my little boy. Even everyday tasks could leave me feeling sore and bloated due to inflammation. This, as you can imagine was frustrating learning to live with the pain every day. I sought NHS and Private advice only to be told that my condition could be rectified with surgery, not available on the NHS as it was now viewed as cosmetic. My heart sank as it was not about how I looked, it was how I felt, and the continuous pain."

"Having been drawn to Paula at the health show I then booked in and had a treatment with the Psychic Surgeons. During the session I felt a fuzzy feeling around my stomach area, and I felt various emotions all of which were calming and soothing. Upon receiving the treatment with Paula and her team of Psychic Surgeons I felt calm and reassured.

Afterwards, I began to notice that as I went about my daily chores I was no longer in pain! I could go swimming and running without being sore and bloated, I was picking my little boy up without even anticipating the pain. Since then, I'm swimming, horse riding and I have even run a half marathon! I simply have been cured and I am now able to live my life as it was. Thank you Paula and your team of Psychic Surgeons you have given me my life back."

Paula's vegetarian choices

In December 2017 I found that I was really struggling with eating meat. I had already cut out eating red meat some time previously and was actually only eating chicken and fish with my fresh vegetables and fruit. But as my own vibration was getting higher and higher it was not appropriate for me to continue to eat meat anymore. With the guidance from the Psychic Surgeons I asked, "Was it time for me to stop eating any meat?" *"Yes"* was their reply. I asked, "Am I still permitted to eat fish?" *"Yes."* I have been meat free in my diet now for the last three years and have adjusted well to becoming pescatarian.

But in recent months I noticed I was not eating as much fish in my diet and knew this was a sign that I was needing to review this. Again, I asked the Psychic Surgeons, "Am I permitted to eat fish anymore?" *"No."* Gosh, that was a shock! No fish, I felt nervous, what was I going to eat instead? I asked the Psychic Surgeons "If I don't eat fish anymore does that make me a vegetarian?" *"Yes."* "Is it your intention for me to become Vegan in the future?" *"Yes."* Oh gosh that's even worse because I'm not really that keen on vegetables. I know it's just a case of adjustment, but I love my food.

I have only withdrawn these foods from my diet because of the work I do with the Psychic Surgeons. I can remember back to the days when I loved a nice steak and chips. I know why the Psychic Surgeons were asking this of me, it's because my vibration is changing and raising higher and higher for our healing work. But it wasn't just removing meat and fish from my diet, I found that I no longer craved fizzy drinks, I was guided to no more coffee, no more dairy, no more bread, the Surgeons have even asked me to stop eating tomatoes! When my microwave broke down and was unrepairable I was guided not to replace it. The Psychic Surgeons no longer wished for me to eat radiated food. As their channel they wanted to keep me healthy.

I am adding this to my successes because it is a massive achievement for me to change the way I am eating. Through the change and increase in my vibration it has changed the healing too, people are reporting just how much stronger it feels. I did ask the Surgeons this question though, "Can I still have my chocolate?" *"Yes."* So there's a bonus...

* Name changed to protect the privacy of this person.

<u>Happy feet</u>
*Jack first approached me after having received a recommendation from a friend about the   wonderful healing that we could offer to him. During our telephone conversation he asked all about the Psychic Surgeons, the healing and could we help him with his recent injury?

Jack had to carefully look after his feet, because of an injury to his foot and a hospital operation. His foot was taking much longer to heal, with pain and swelling around the surgery site. After weeks of convalescing he was still unable to get around without any foot pain. I asked the Psychic Surgeons for their guidance and they guided me that we could assist Jack in offering him the distant healing sessions only, as Jack lived over ninety miles away.

I had already asked Jack to provide me with a full length photograph of himself as this is how the Psychic Surgeons connect to a patient. In addition to this photo, Jack very kindly provided me with a photograph of just his feet. His right foot looked very red, angry and swollen.
After the Psychic Surgeons had sent their distant healing to Jack, I emailed him with some feedback from the session. The Psychic Surgeons needed to clear mental blockages from his mind.

These were not only the day to day stresses and mental blockages but also from the trauma he had gone through with his health condition.

As this was Jack's first ever healing session there were many suppressed emotions to be released from his heart chakra. These emotions if not released, were blocking him from moving forward in life (literally) and stopping his body from healing itself. The Psychic Surgeons then worked to give healing to Jack's foot and toes, removing the blocked energy from around those areas and reviewing the hospital surgery that had taken place on his right foot. The Psychic Surgeons had also needed to give healing to his right knee, as Jack had been walking differently to protect his right foot in the months following his operation.

Jack reported back, "I felt a big rush of heat on my face and a strong colour purple behind my eyes. I felt very calm and warm today. My foot got quite warm for a little while. I could feel wiggling in my toes and had lots of tingling in my hands. My whole body is buzzing! My foot feels a lot better thank you. It's not clear yet but the pain is much much less."

A gap of six months passed before Jack got in contact again. Jack reported, "My foot has been doing well and I feel it is actually fully healed now. (No it is not). I am just left with some swelling which is affecting the structure of my foot and how I use it." Based upon this feedback from Jack I was guided by the Psychic Surgeons to restart the distant healing sessions.

After each healing session Jack reported, how calm he felt in his mind, the anxiety he had from his foot condition just melted away by the Psychic Surgeons. But the path back to Jack's wellness was so up and down.

It literally was one step forward and two steps back. When Jack reported, "My foot has been doing really well...until the last two weeks where it has felt a bit unsettled and quite a bit of pain in my toes as well...it definitely needs the healing."

A few weeks later he informed me he had completed a long walk in a new pair of shoes causing pain in both of his feet. Then the following weekend he managed to walk into the leg of the coffee table bashing his left foot and bruising it. Ouch! The Psychic Surgeons assured me, "We are making progress with Jack's feet." The distant healing sessions continued for Jack but on a more structured and more regular basis, so that he was easily able to get out and about. Jack reported, "Thank you so much for the healing sessions it really has made a big difference."

As the weeks progressed, I asked Jack if he would take a new photograph of his feet, same pose, same background, as I was sure that there would be a difference in the 'before and after' photos for me to see. The difference between the first photograph and the second photograph were incredible. Jack commented, "This is how my feet look right now, as you can see the right foot is so much less angry than before, I can't believe the change in colour! I'm so happy and grateful for everything you have done. Truly."

In the following distant healing session, the Psychic Surgeons guided me that they wanted to use the new photograph of Jack's feet only, and not his full length photograph. In this particular healing session there were five Psychic Surgeons in total giving the healing to Jack and three of the Surgeons were working on his feet. In the feedback to Jack I reported that the Psychic Surgeons worked on and gave healing on the right foot 'hospital operation' area, the right foot big toe, then the length of the foot, all down the instep of the right foot to the right ankle, then up the right calf and then up to and concentrating on and around the right knee.

The left foot received healing to the toes, the ball of the left foot, the ankle and left knee. Healing was also given to his lower back and hips. Jack replied, "My foot has been amazing so much better. The best it has been for the last three months!"

The distant healing has continued to this present day, allowing Jack to continue to walk comfortably without pain.

Jack's own words: "You really have changed my life! I'm so grateful and in awe of what you do, after each session, everything just seems that little bit more possible. Thanks again for everything you do."

Babies

In recent years I have been approached by different ladies wishing to conceive a child but without any success. Some had tried IVF and failed. Others have wanted to naturally add to their family and could not. The Psychic Surgeons have been amazing in their success for infertility, although I need to add, it may not be successful for everyone. To date we have been able to help bring five baby girls and one baby boy with another baby on its way into this world!

From Book to Distant Healing

"What a very interesting read. Your book was everything I thought it would be and more! I was so gripped by Paula's real life story that I read more than I planned the first evening, and it was well past my bedtime before I would put it down! I couldn't resist having some psychic surgery healing for myself from Paula and the Psychic Surgeons as I was about to go through a major operation, the removal of a huge ovarian cyst plus a hysterectomy. Prior to my hospital operation I was told that the scan revealed something that I hoped it wasn't, and before your psychic surgery healing the consultant surgeon said there was a possibility of cancer that was showing up on the scan."

"She even mentioned in the advanced stages, although they wouldn't know for sure until they operated on me. I kept positive and had great faith that all would be well."

"You and the Surgeons carried out the distant Psychic Surgeons healing. In the operation they did find cancer but, it was all contained within the cyst and in the early stages, I think the consultant said stage 2. Therefore nothing was left inside my body as it was all taken away when they cut out the cyst. All other tests were clear!"

"The evening after my operation, the hospital surgeon revealed that the operation had gone better than expected, and nothing untoward was found (much to my relief.) She also said that they wouldn't know for sure until the results had come back from the lab. I continued with some more distant healing sessions after my operation."

"Well my recovery was really fast, and I feel absolutely fantastic and even more so today as my results have revealed a load of positives and taken any niggling doubts away."

"Thank you so much Paula and the Psychic Surgeons, I am totally convinced that your help played a big part in my brilliant recovery. Above all else I think what you and the Psychic Surgeons did is absolutely remarkable! I feel the best I've felt in years and back to my old self.
Thanks again Paula, you are a real star, and the Psychic Surgeons are amazing, please give them my love and sincere gratitude."

Distant Healing Feedback

"After my distant healing sessions with the Psychic Surgeons, I wanted to let you know, I got sensations all over my body at various times. I felt like something was taken out of my chest and immediately felt the relief after. My chest, back and stomach were worked on again. I could feel the sensation. When it was over, I felt like I had come out of a deep dream and that I had travelled and was a little dazed. It took me longer than normal to come to my senses. Now, I'm feeling really great and balanced. It was just as wonderful as last week, if not more so. During the distant healing session I had the same metallic taste in my mouth again to begin with which eventually went. My chest area was worked on again with immense warmth. But this time my back and stomach were also worked. I can still feel the warmth in my chest. Thank you."

The Hospital Update. – see below

"I spoke with my consultant on Wednesday. They are very pleased with the results of my last scan which was a week before Easter. Everything is looking the same as the last very positive result, which was the lump in my chest had reduced dramatically and that there was now just a tiny spot on my liver. She said the spot on my liver looks even better this time round! They aren't that particularly concerned about the abnormality in my neck/back region anymore because the last scan was showing no activity and what was there looks like its scarring over! So all's very positive and very different from when you did my first session with me."

"I've always been spiritual in nature and I've studied healing although I don't practice it as such. Mainly because I just can't seem to figure out which direction to take. So when I was diagnosed with this type of cancer and told there was no cure. I rejected chemo as I wasn't having any debilitating symptoms and felt that chemo would ruin any quality of life I had left. Well that was the best decision I could have made. I was offered immunotherapy which is a lot less aggressive, and I've been responding remarkably well with it."

"I have a friend who is also a practicing spiritual healer and she was giving me regular healing. During one of her sessions she wondered whether I might have been a Psychic Surgeon or something like that in a past life and suggested I did some research on it and that's how I found you!"

"So my long winded answer is yes. I do feel the Psychic Surgeons have been instrumental in the success of my treatment, along with a very positive mindset and daily meditations." xx

* Name changed to protect the privacy of this person.

Stomach cancer

I recently heard from *Philippa a lady patient, who had received the Psychic Surgeons healing both in person and distant healing. Her condition was stomach cancer, and the Psychic Surgeons were very active in their healing of her condition. A decision needed to be made by Philippa when the hospital advised the stomach was to be removed. The Psychic Surgeons were against this removal and I let Philippa know we could help her through the healing, but it would take some time. I knew through her family pressure that she just wanted to get 'it' taken out and I was not surprised by her decision to go ahead with the operation and have her stomach removed.

Some months later, I enquired as to how she was and how was she coping after the stomach operation? This was her reply.
"I've been really well. The doctors think I'm amazing and I feel very well most of the time. Of course there are the occasional drops in blood sugar and me eating too much, but generally I'm getting on well. I am starting my own Nutrition business, writing a book for those going through stomach cancer and gastrectomy's."

"Also I meant to tell you that when they did my pathology it came back with a "complete" result. The tumour had 'reverted' to scar tissue and all the lymph nodes were clear.

So I didn't need to have the operation after all!

But unfortunately they (the hospitals) are 20 years away from a test that can show that. I think my stomach was a weak point and I feel stronger without it. Anyway an interesting journey."

Paula asked: "Do you put the 'complete' result down to the healing from the Psychic Surgeons? Do you think you would be where you are today without their healing?"

Philippa replied, "I think it was a combination of everything but yes, the Psychic Surgeons definitely were a major part."

* Name changed to protect the privacy of this person.

Head injury

In early December 2020 I was contacted to ask if an urgent appointment could be made to send distant healing to a lady in New Zealand who had had an accident the previous weekend. She had fractured her skull in the accident and had a two hour hospital operation. Her outlook was that she was now recovering but expected to be in Rehab for some time to come.

The very next day the distant healing was arranged to be sent and with the thirteen hour time difference the lady called *Leigh, would be fast asleep in her hospital bed to receive the healing from the Psychic Surgeons. The Neurosurgeon from the Psychic Surgeons Team came forward as the main Surgeon to perform the healing. Giving healing to her brain due to the accident and impact trauma, then healing to the hospital surgery site and then to the head stitches and healing of the skin. Mentally the Neurosurgeon removed mental blockages from Leigh.

As expected some stress and anxiety they found were removed from deep within her mind.

Other Surgeons from the Team of Psychic Surgeons then stepped forward and worked deep in her heart chakra to clear the emotions and trauma of the accident.

Then physically, in addition to the head wound healing, the Psychic Surgeons detected that healing was needed to her neck, her shoulders and down the length of her spine, all of which, took the impact of her accident. I was guided by the Psychic Surgeons to let her family know that one more distant healing session would be required in three weeks.

The family replied "Oh wow, thank you Paula that sounds like a hugely productive and beneficial session. So very grateful to you and the Surgeons, I will pass on any feedback to you on her improvement. A million thank you's."

A day after the distant healing had been sent, feedback arrived saying that Leigh was much livelier and more awake and more talkative and happier in herself which the family were heartened to see.

On the second day after the distant healing had been sent, more feedback arrived by email.

"Just as you said, she's healing more day by day it's just wonderful. The family have been given permission to take her out for a spin out into the fresh air and a bit of sunshine, which she enjoyed. Super perky this morning.....partly due to another marathon sleep! But everything is much improved, pain way lower, scar healing nicely according to the hospital Surgeon."

Six days after sending the distant healing
Leigh was slightly improved until she went to the hospital rehab and it has freaked her out and caused her quite a bit of anxiety. She had assessments, saw Doctors, had physio and a gym session.

Further assessments the following day, then to figure out a plan and timeframe for her stay.

They were letting her home on the Friday for the weekend. (Back on Monday possibly) Then hopefully back home for a few days over Christmas. The Psychic Surgeons had indicated that being at home would be better for her healing and recovery and be more effective in her own home.

Twelve days after sending the distant healing
The family wrote, "Just wanted to keep you in the loop, as Leigh was allowed home for the weekend. There is to be a family meeting with the hospital staff to get the recovery 'programme'.... Seeing her at home, she'll be out in no time. She already thinks she's healed!"

Thirteen days after sending the distant healing (23rd December)
The family reported, "Leigh is home tomorrow for good! That's a great Christmas present for us all. What an incredible speedy turnaround it's been, I have no doubt at all that the Surgeons and you played a huge part in that. I'm so grateful."
Paula replied, "To receive your wonderful email is a delight. I am so pleased for her and your family, it's been such a worrying time for them all, but not anymore. The healing from the Psychic Surgeons is truly wonderful and for the healing to reach all around to the other side of the world to New Zealand still blows my mind. She has responded beautifully to their healing and now she is spending Christmas at home, just perfect."

The follow up appointment was booked with Paula, and the Psychic Surgeons sent a second distant healing to Leigh three weeks after the first session.
Paula reported that, "The distant healing from the Psychic Surgeons had been sent and they had again worked deep in her brain, her head, her mind to heal and rebalance."

"Then healing to her heart chakra to release more emotions. Physically the Psychic Surgeons gave healing to her head, to the site of her hospital operation, again to both sides of her neck and then across both shoulders."

The feedback from the family has been incredible. The family wrote:
"Leigh is doing so well, with healthcare people making home visits and running memory tests on her. She has been given the go ahead to start a brand new job at the end of January 2021 (part time only) and Leigh is thrilled to be able to fulfil this obligation. It seems quite incredible when we think how she was just a month ago! Thank you."

5. The Psychic Surgeons

I am delighted to share with you 'the Light that is in my Life', and that is another twelve portraits of the Psychic Surgeons from the Collective that is known as the Psychic Surgeons Team. All of these Psychic Surgeons work regularly through my hands. At the time of writing my first book, Journal of a Psychic Surgeon, there were twenty-two different Psychic Surgeons working in the Team carrying out the Psychic Surgeons healing. Twelve of those twenty-two Psychic Surgeons came forward to be drawn and their portraits can be found in my first book.

Now, as I write this second book in 2021, I have received confirmation from the Psychic Surgeons themselves, that there are now fifty-five Psychic Surgeons working through my hands! Not all at the same time, because I asked, "Do ALL of the Psychic Surgeons have the opportunity to work through me on a regular basis?" "*Yes*" they replied.

Even though this is all happening to me, I am still so in awe of my connection to the Psychic Surgeons and what is being accomplished. To have been chosen in this way, to have so many eminent Surgeons coming forward, to be able to continue their work in this way is such an honour. As their channel I have been gifted the responsibility of promoting what we do, I am their 'front man' so to speak, sharing with people the incredible Psychic Surgeon healing that is being carried out daily. I am representing The Psychic Surgeon Team, at events and shows, on social media and through my books to increase people's awareness of their Psychic Surgeons healing. The images of the Psychic Surgeons are shown as numbered portraits with each of the Psychic Surgeon's descriptions and information on the pages that follow.

7

8

9

10

11

12

51

The Psychic Surgeons:

Drawing number one is:
1) Dr Ender – Psychic Surgeon, he is from Bodrum in Turkey from the 18th Century. He assists Paula with grounding patients through Divine Light from the Soul Star chakra through to the Earth chakra, allowing for the patient to be grounded to keep them in their body during a healing session. He also helps with mental health, with depression, anxiety, and addictions. To alleviate the addictions of any Mental Health problems, he will uplift, align, and ground the system to be anchored into. A direct connection to The Source, energy light. As he works through Paula her hands will be 'Ariel' above the patient. He uses pink and blue healing energy. Imagine a 'whoosh' of crystalline light, that's what he will be bringing through as well as grounding. He is a humble man and came forward in March 2019.

2) Dr Thekchen - is a Tibetan gentleman (wears his hair long in a plait says there is energy in long hair,) and he lived on earth in the 18th century. He comes forward to assist with the healing of the whole gastro-intestinal area, from the top of the stomach (solar plexus down to the base chakra.) He radiates orange light over all this area of the Sacral chakra. He works in the abdominal area, on intensive conditions, ulcerations, and the gynaecological area. He had his own private practice and was a Surgeon in his own right, dealing with the women's reproductive systems, a gynaecologist performing caesarean sections. For the patient he will be helping the flow of energy in between these chakra areas, and on the physical to heal and comfort. He is connected with two other Psychic Surgeons when working, that of El Moyra (Ascended Master) and also a Surgeon of the highest crystalline light. When they work together a beautiful pyramid is created to amplify the healing energy further, delivering exactly what is needed for the patient at that time.

Holding the space in the ethers for Dr Thekchen and the Ascended Master to feed through even higher, lighter refined healing energy. Dr Thekchen lived in a small village at the foot of the Tibetan mountain range with only a handful of other people around him. And he was the one to ensure everyone received the nourishment they needed. He is showing the importance of a nourishing diet including lots of vegetables as it is this food that 'radiates' out to every part of the body, it is these gifts and inner knowledge he wishes to bring to the patients.

3) Dr Chkeeto pronounced Ch-kee-to is a medicine man/Shaman and he lived 700 years ago. He lived in Sao Paulo in Eastern Brazil before the deforestation of the Amazon when all was in balance. As a highly evolved spiritual Shaman he brings the gift of healing, he is able to move blockages. He has an abundance of knowledge related to the mind, body and soul. Mental health problems such as depression, anxiety and trauma. Also, physical ailments such as joint pain, libido and overall health. He is a wonderful guide, a kind empathic man with a good sense of humour (a vibrant soul) offering guidance and protection, healing, and his love from Divine Source.

Appearing in his portrait in his 50's he is very lean and muscular, he is adorned with a bright coloured feather headdress. He had a large 'lip plate' on his bottom lip, (to show his standing in the community) pierced ears with feathers through.

The knowledge he had, was handed down to him from his predecessors. His job was to assist in ceremonies such as the coming of age, births, deaths, along with rituals to assist in one's spiritual growth. His ancestral apothecary (he was a person who prepared medicine or drugs). He was surrounded by nature, there was a treasure trove of medicinal plants, shrubs, flowers, root, bark, berries, leaves and herbs. Even the use of insects and animals had healing properties. Some plants were very hard to find due to certain times of the year and their location.

He was able to create antiseptics, pain relief, and other ointments to treat a wide variety of ailments. He marvelled at the pure raw ingredients and their effects on the body and the mind. He truly cared for the people in his community and with the difficulties he faced when dealing with a hopeless situation. For example, deaths of young children or stillbirths he hated how it made him feel so he remembered his successes. He took his medical knowledge with him back to the spirit realm where he continues to build on his skills. He now has a greater understanding of what works and what does not.

He is so pleased to be working with you Paula and the Psychic Surgeon Team, he has fitted in very nicely and is well respected by the other Psychic Surgeons.

4) Dr Dunot of Saint-Maclou, Normandy, (1828-1891) became known as The Doctor of the Lourdes Grotto. He had looked after other people all of his life and after the death of his wife he dedicated his work to helping the sick. He established in 1883 the Bureau of Medical Observations in Lourdes. He was the founder and first president of the Bureau which was called upon to investigate reports of inexplicable healing. He felt his new 'calling' was from the Virgin Mary at Lourdes. It is my understanding that the Bureau reviewed up to fifty cases a year of 'unexpected cures'. He helped to differentiate between receiving a grace and receiving a miracle (that which is without any scientific explanation on the basis of current medical knowledge) this result was then presented to and certified by a Catholic Bishop and recognised as miraculous.

5) Dr George Smith - this Psychic Surgeon has carried out all sorts of surgery. Ears, Nose and Throat, the brain, extracted teeth, dentistry, amputation (which he did not like). He was a real gentleman. American by birth but with English ancestors and with connections to Wales.

He had been to France and the United Kingdom when he was a young man. He was trained as an Ear, Nose and Throat Surgeon which he was very passionate about and loved.

He was of service in the forces in the American Civil War, 1861-1865, in Kentucky USA as a Field Surgeon. With poor working conditions in a makeshift tent he was working on the floor with patients. He had his surgical instruments laid out; blunt instruments, non-sterilised instruments, he could not get his hands on any brandy to sterilise the instruments. His main job was to perform amputations as well as removing shrapnel and bullets. Men's lives rested in his hands, he had to work under great pressure making on the spot life-saving decisions and having to deal with blood loss and gangrene and infection which took many men's lives. He had good steady hands and good concentration to achieve the best outcome for his patients. He was a brave soul who saved many lives. His own passing was very quick. He was shot by the enemy, taken from behind and was unaware of it. It was a part of his life that he absolutely hated, he did not like to amputate.

He is very happy to be working with you Paula and has been around you since the 15th of July 2019, when you were travelling to France. You are going to start working with patients who have problems with their mouth or throat issues, and will be very drawn to teeth, dentistry, ears nose and throat. (Yes we are!)

6) Dr Andrew (Andy) Davies was from the era of the 1970's. He is a Colorectal Surgeon specialising in bowel disorders of the rectum, anus and colon. He was English and from the North of England. He was a specialist in his field. He is in his mid-50s in the drawing and has been working with Paula for the last two years. This drawing was channeled to Paula and as the image was created on the page, she let the Psychic Surgeon artist use her own hands to complete the drawing of this Surgeon's portrait.

7) Dr Nantez was a Surgeon who lived within the Mayan civilisation over 4,000 years ago in the country of Belize in Central America. He was known for his alchemy in transmuting matter and the study of astrology, the sun, the moon and the planets were and are very important. In that time he was an elevated Being, playing with light energy and healing people in this way. He used sound to heal with the power of vibration and sound frequency. He was very stylish, and cared about his appearance, but was reserved, modest and shy.

Today as he works through Paula, he works from the throat chakra. His purpose is to bring out the point of truth for physical problems like throat cancer. To bring alignment to ailments of the throat. He is conscious for each of us to pay attention to our words that are spoken, we must articulate with clarity. He says, "We must clean up our act on what we say to each other". Vibration is everything, the voice has a vibration to it. He is a messenger to this world. He does not come alone; he has his own Team of Surgeons. He marvels at our human ways. Each person has their own vibration. People will learn from being ill. They have lost their confidence to listen to their inner voice, they are out of balance with themselves. He is here to change the world, he brings vibration into the world, to be of service.

8) Dr Ling is a Heart Surgeon. A modern day Surgeon from the 1970's. He wears a long white jacket, and he holds a clip board. He is Chinese, but he spent some years in America and also in England. He has a lovely nature and light-hearted energy. He brings with him a feeling of joy, happiness, and a motivated energy. Bringing the colours of the rainbow and upon seeing these colours the vibrations raise higher and higher.

He is practicing modern medicine and modern practices. It is reconstructive surgery of the heart, the heart begins to build a white energy and in energy form, shows all the connections made to the heart.

He very much appreciates the Teamwork of the Psychic Surgeons as they work together to perform the psychic surgery. When working as the lead expert this Surgeon is also the main communicator during the surgery. As he overshadows Paula, he says "He is in the driver's seat." He was completely focused with his work, and he had strong and firm boundaries. He learned that the hard way, he was too work focused when he was younger, yes, he excelled in his work, but he did not spend much of his youth living.

He says, "Balance is very important in all aspects of everything." Dr Ling insists that we are all a Team and that includes their channel, Paula.
His message to us all, "He says, keep the happiness, keep the kindness, the laughter... keep that flowing, it is what the world needs right now."

9) Dr Jacob – Obstetrician Psychic Surgeon came forward, showing himself as a tall slim upright man. He was wearing a grey suit with quite a long jacket. He also showed himself dressed in a white coat when he was working as a Surgeon, this fastened at the shoulder and was calf length and much fuller. He has been working through Paula for the last three years.

He was Swiss and from the era of the 19th century. As he grew up, he had a fascination with precision instruments and had access to them. There may have been clockmakers in his family. He used these instruments to make and mend things like his toys. He valued the instruments and would ensure they were returned to their proper place and in pristine condition. His toys would be well maintained and even performance enhanced! With a very enquiring mind, he would perform post-mortems on birds or squirrels that he found dead in the countryside. He did this discretely and the animal remains would be analysed and documented before being securely disposed of.

He came from privilege and trained as a physician in Obstetrics helping many women. He had a fascination for '2 lives in one' and in particular studied the gestation period and growth of the foetus. He was a 'truth seeker' and a problem solver. He would irritate his colleagues when long after they gave up on a patient as being impossible to help, he would still be pouring over books or trying experiments to find a solution.

Dr Jacob is a man who is extremely fastidious maybe even OCD. He kept his surgery tools pristine and would be angry if they were not where they should be. He would also have tools made if he saw the need for them. He understood to some degree the importance for cleanliness and germs, something that was not always common practice when he was working. Although his temperament may have irritated those around him it was for the greater good, health and welfare of those who came to see him.

Now in spirit Dr Jacob is a hard task master and will encourage Paula to persevere with difficult cases. He will be the one who gets her to think 'outside' of the box if something is not progressing as she might expect. He also steps in to give Paula strength in her wellbeing or in her work situations. He acts as your professional moderator and his standards are high, and he can be brusque at times when trying to get the job done.

Dr Jacob does have a soft centre and will metaphorically put his arm around Paula when she's had a tough day. He says he is very proud of her achievements, (but he says don't let this go to your head!)
The turquoise background of his portrait is indictive of the power and pureness of the healing generated through this man and his link to Source.

10) Dr Azim, Psychic Surgeon specialises in Haematology, disorders of the blood. Born in India in the 1870's. This wise, quietly spoken and mild mannered spiritual individual has been working through Paula for the last three years. Very 'matter of fact' about his work, he tells that without blood we do not function, and unhealthy blood can damage other parts of the body. As well as dealing with the blood and kidney related disorders his focus is also to balance and heal the base chakra. His thought processes are simplistic and logical. Things are what they are, and he has no damaging ego. He does what he is guided to do for the greater good.

11) Dr Li – Psychic Surgeon has been working through Paula for the last eight years. He makes his presence known to her by a tingling sensation on the side of her face and also a slight ringing sound in her inner ear with a ticklish feel. He is small in stature and dressed in a cream coloured robe. He practiced Taoism; an ancient tradition of philosophy and religious belief deeply rooted in Chinese customs. It promotes achieving harmony or union with nature. The three virtues of Taoism are: 1) Compassion, Kindness and Love. 2) Moderation, Simplicity and Frugality. And finally, 3) Humility and Modesty.

Dr Li was a medicine man using apothecary for his tinctures, and preparations. He shows the use of herbs, medicines, and scales. The right amount of each makes the perfect medicine he says and nods. He speaks of old and new methods, and how it all fits together. He resided in a very 'old style' oriental building where he served the community with his healing. He lived his earthly life in ancient China a very, very, long time ago, in the 4th century BC, he says and chuckles. He has a warm, bright smile. He has a very loving, and friendly nature. Kind, and patient and very understanding. He was married and had 2 children.

He helps the other Psychic Surgeons with energy healing but also in the making of products in a physical form, tincture type bottles. He says it's important for people to feel good on the inside as well as the outside. He wants to take positive steps and action to help create better and happier people.

Dr Li now talks of the world at present, the cleansing that is taking place, the healing, and how it has had the 'Band-Aid' pulled off of it. Wounds left open to heal he says and nods.
Lots of people need little steps with kindness, and he points to dear Paula with this, he says "You are very kind and understanding of people and their needs."
He nods gently and he says of Paula, "You are blessed, there are many new journeys beginning." Dr Li is a very beautiful Psychic Surgeon with a wealth of knowledge.

12) Sir Harold Delf Gillies OBE FRCS - was an Otolaryngologist and pioneer in the ground-breaking, innovative procedures in plastic surgery and who, is still widely considered to be the father of modern day plastic surgery. His work marked the dawn of innovative procedures in plastic surgery as we know it today.
Born in 1882 in New Zealand he served in the Army during the First World War and was able to help the wounded soldiers with his reconstructive surgery. After WW1 he was later based in London. He married and had 4 children. He loved the outdoor pursuits of rowing and golf. He is shown here in his portrait around the age of thirty-five.
With an outwardly serious manner, Dr Gillies was someone who was highly intelligent and brilliant in his field, he did not suffer fools gladly and could be quite brusque. But those who got to know him well always attested to the fact that he was a fair and generous friend to have, and who always put the care and health of his patients to be paramount.

Dr Gillies was known for his innovative reconstructive plastic surgery and carried out many procedures that had not been attempted before. He also specialised in sex reassignment surgery. His first plastic surgery was carried out in 1917 where he developed a new method of facial reconstructive surgery. After WW1 he helped the disfigured soldiers, reconstructing their faces. He set up the world's first ever hospital dedicated to the treatment of facial injuries at the Queen Mary's Hospital in Sidcup Kent developing many state of the art techniques of plastic surgery. For his war services he was knighted in 1930. He had his own private practice and travelled extensively, lecturing, teaching and promoting the most advanced techniques in the world. During WW2 and afterwards he trained many doctors from the Commonwealth nations in plastic surgery. He died in 1960 at the age of 78.

When working with Paula he wants everything to be geared towards the patient, at the same time performing to his own exacting standards from all those in the spirit Psychic Surgeons Team.

~ ~ ~ ~ ~

Where known, I want to share with you some of the other 'new' Psychic Surgeons who have joined the Team who work through me and have made their presence known together with their medical specialities.

This is what is called a 'Bank of Psychic Surgeons'. There are no images of these Psychic Surgeons to show you, some may come forward as and when it is appropriate in the future to be seen or drawn. Some of the information on a Psychic Surgeon that has been given, may be sparse in detail, but these needed to be shared as these Psychic Surgeons work through me to do the Psychic Surgeon healing.

The Bank of Psychic Surgeons

Dr Mohammed Usaff – He was a General Surgeon, and had an interest in growths, maybe tumours, cysts, or lymphomas, not necessarily cancer. During a healing session he uses Paula's fingers like lasers. He is from Saudi Arabia and was a more modern-day Doctor. There are three other Surgeons in the Team who also work this way with Paula's fingers. He was on this earth plane when lasers were just being designed in 1970's or 80's. He had cancer when he passed, he wanted the Doctors to practice on him, but they never could, it was too dangerous. Dr Usaff is fascinated by the spiritual healing, and he is still learning himself in his own field.

The Professor – A Neurosurgeon. He deals with the neurological system for patients. He is another eminent Surgeon coming forward to join the Team. A much more intense energy with this new Neurosurgeon. This gentleman is a much younger energy now with Paula and he is much more knowledgeable, I need to say, he is very well respected.

He is of good standing, a strong energy and Paula will feel that change, you will feel the need to work differently. Known as The Professor. He has been around you when working with the Lady with the brain tumour. Really strong man, very strong energy about him, intense energy with him, he wants to reassure you, he says "You feel the boundaries are being pushed so far with the work that you are doing, and please appreciate, we know you are working on the earth plane and its constraints, do not worry we have your back, we are stepping up a gear with you."

Dr David – Psychic Surgeon - Came forward in November 2019. He works on the bones, specialises on the skeleton. He has a Canadian accent where he originated.

He then came and worked in the UK. He is quite small in stature with pointed features, and a large nose. Thin features/lean. He wears ½ glasses in silver. Has wavy/ frizzy strawberry blond coloured hair and pointy fingers and is a serious person.

Dr Dellucci – A new Psychic Surgeon who came forward in October 2019. From Columbia. He had his own practice but not in hospitals. He works on hands and wrists up to the elbow. His era was 1950's when he died.

Dr Patel – Psychic Surgeon was a modern-day general Surgeon. But also served in the Military as a Military Surgeon. He worked in the NHS and specialised in the Spinal cord; he talks about trauma in a patient in an accident after losing the use of limbs downwards. He likes to study the brain, meningitis and spinal cord inflammation, how it works. The swelling of the brain, the spinal cord and nasal cavities. He was a modern-day Surgeon in shirt and trousers, a Consultant, he was also an Anaesthetist. An Indian gentleman and a very very, intelligent man. He says, "He never thought he would be doing this sort of thing, Spiritual type of work!" He is very much into this now and very interested, and he is learning. He is part of the Surgical Team. He is fascinated by all the Psychic Surgeon minds together. He used to work with children in Paediatrics. He is in the Psychic Surgeons Team to oversee, to put in a modern twist of his experience to the other Psychic Surgeons of what he knows. He is not changing how Paula works, he is not going to be overwhelming, more of a presence. He has a sense of humour. He was taken quite young, that's why he wants to continue his work in Spirit. A smell of latex around you Paula will let you know its him, he is not going to be the biggest presence in the Team but, will be in the middle of the Surgical Group whilst operating.

Psychic Surgeon – of Vibrational healing – A very smart man coming forward in July 2019, he is linked to the late 1700's to early 1800's and linked to music, orchestras, music in that way, a link to sound waves and energy levels. We all give off energy, and illnesses give off energies. The Surgeon is coming in as an additional help to the Psychic Surgeons to work to increase the wavelength of that healing vibration.

Paula won't necessarily be seeing or feeling him a lot, her hands may shake a bit more when he has stepped in; when something is more deeply rooted in the patient that we may not know about, he will step in when a greater vibration is needed. He will be using sound waves and hitting the problem area. He is saying "To let Paula know if you do things a little differently, it is he who is coming in to help."

Ship's Surgeon – No name given – The Surgeon steps forward showing an image of the ship, The Mary Rose. (Paula had just visited the Mary Rose exhibition, in Portsmouth's Historic Dockyard, in June of 2019, where she took photographs of the Mary Rose ship's Surgeons equipment, during her visit).

There is a Surgeon linked to the Mary Rose who will be helping you now because of you going there to see the Mary Rose. When the Psychic Surgeons saw that you went there to The Mary Rose ship, the new Surgeon came forward and linked in with this connection. The Ship's Surgeon was a man of science and wore a head covering called a coif, which was lined with silk to show he had served a seven-year apprenticeship under a Master Surgeon. He is showing one of the many tools he used, a Surgeons saw. The Surgeon is showing that he heated up the saw to sterilise it to perform amputations.

Other tools used were, a knife, a razor, a tourniquet, needles, scissors, clamps and bandages and lint. This is the Psychic Surgeon helping you now. He is quite tall with shirt sleeves rolled back, blood over his arms.

He comes to bring you into the history of Surgery, wants you to learn the history, going back to Roman times of how they did surgery, he wants you to see how far ahead the Romans were, their knowledge of scurvy, knowledge of Vitamin C.

Understand the knowledge of that, to understand what the Psychic Surgeons are doing and what they are aiming to do, so that you have the background of everything. To eventually understand the transition of Surgery.

The Ship's Surgeon had to perform operations and be a dentist and a pharmacist too. Some of the conditions he had to treat were, fevers such as yellow fever, malaria, even the plague. Venereal disease, lung disease, dysentery, rickets, scurvy, parasites as well as treating work related injuries and battle wounds.

Lady Psychic Surgeons – Although none of the female Psychic Surgeons who work within the Team have come forward to be drawn or mentioned, I have been assured that they are definitely there working with me on a regular basis. As you know there is a very large Team of 55 Psychic Surgeons that work through me and I asked how many were female Psychic Surgeons? I have been guided that there are fifteen female Psychic Surgeons, and I am so pleased to know this and to acknowledge their presence.

I hope you have enjoyed reading about the incredible Psychic Surgeons. They are all very accomplished, dedicated and also have a good sense of humour. It is a delight for me to work with this wonderful Team and the close relationship I have with them, I am so blessed.

6. My Spiritual Journeys

Before I had completed writing my first book Journal of a Psychic Surgeon, I had received a message in a clairvoyant reading from the Psychic Surgeons in July 2017 that they wished me to visit Brazil in South America. The person giving me the message did not know the relevance of this message, but I did. I knew it was to do with the world-renowned Psychic Surgeon healer, John of God. I had watched many of his videos on the internet of his Psychic Surgery healing at his healing centre, The Casa Healing Centre in Abadiania, Central Brazil.

I asked, "Was I to travel there to observe him or to receive healing?" and the Psychic Surgeons replied *"Both, we want you to go to observe him working in the physical, see it. We want you to gain as much knowledge as possible. The reason you are being guided to visit John of God is because he is very much going to support your channel. There will be initiations, there will be symbols; medical divine symbols, divine symbols of science that are 'other worldly' that you will receive. There will be healing for you that cannot be given to you anywhere else in the world except Brazil."* Wow!

The Psychic Surgeons continued, *"The sheer power with John of God of spirituality in this place is something that will anchor your healing channel further within your being, more than ever before that you are not quite achieving here in the UK. So, there is a reason for you to be guided to go there and this will be very soon. So that your healing will evolve and transform into more than it was before."*

My initial euphoria upon hearing this news was soon to leave me when questions started in my mind, how on earth do I begin arranging something like this?

Where in Brazil is his Healing Centre? Who will I be travelling with? How am I going to get there? I had some savings put by and knew that it would be an expensive trip to make so now it was just a case of doing some research on the internet to see what this adventure entailed. And then as if Spirit were trying to help me, the synchronicities started to happen.

In the August of 2017, a friend invited me to go with her to a meditation evening in Glastonbury which I thought was really nice of her, but it would seem that more was to unfold. As we arrived at Goddess House in Glastonbury, we were greeted at the door by a lady dressed all in white. She was the facilitator for the evening but more than that I was informed that she was actually a guide for John of God. Who knew? She had been visiting Brazil for the last seven years as a guide to take people to meet John of God. I was very excited to talk to her so after the evenings meditation finished, I asked her if I may quiz her with several questions about Brazil, how to get there, the cost etc. I was delighted. I thought I had found the person who was going to assist me in getting to Brazil and to meet John of God. Well no, that wasn't the case, I asked the Psychic Surgeons to confirm if she was the correct guide to travel with? *"No."* Oh, well that put the cat amongst the pigeons, now what should I do? I left it for a little while. There was no rush I was told in my original reading that I didn't need to travel Brazil for at least a year to eighteen months and so I did not pursue things further.

Later in August, I visited another friend and during the evening we talked about my possible visit to Brazil. She connected to Spirit and then to the Psychic Surgeons and through her connection they gave her a message to confirm that my presence was needed in Brazil sooner rather than later.

Then in the October I was talking to a new acquaintance about my possible visit to Brazil and she went onto the internet and looked up John of God, she clicked on a photograph of him and kept this on her mobile phone. Then using her hand, linked in with the energy of John of God. This amazed me, I didn't know this could be done. She then gave me a message to say, "He sends a spirit messenger to you this evening who says 'He' knows you are coming." OMG! John of God knows I'm coming to Brazil? I'm going to have to get a move on.

Doing internet research in the November of 2017 I asked the Psychic Surgeons "Do I need to book my flights yet?" *"No."* "Do I book my guide yet?" *"No."* If I am not travelling with a female guide should I look to travel to Brazil with a gentleman?" *"Yes."* This was easy research to do as I had now found the John of God website and a list of international guides with whom you could book to travel with. There were several gentlemen guides to choose from, but the Psychic Surgeons guided me that I was to book with Robert a guide with many years' experience in Brazil with John of God.

It was now December and I was very busy with healing appointments with the Psychic Surgeons, but on one such healing appointment I was busy channeling for the Psychic Surgeons when suddenly the face of John of God appeared in front of me. He was smiling at me, I couldn't believe my eyes and of course I recognised him straight away, in my mind I said, "Hello John of God" and with that my hands (which had been working over the patient on the treatment table) were raised up in the air and cupped my face, he was greeting me. I thanked him, and in my mind told him I was coming to Brazil (as if he didn't know.) He smiled again and then he was gone. Straight away I told my friend and she linked up to Spirit and gave me the following message, "That he was lonely, no one was giving him any healing.

69

He was watching you and how you work with the Psychic Surgeons so different to how he works, she thinks that when you go to Brazil it will be to give him healing." (Little did we know.)

In the January of 2018, I met up with a lady who had already travelled to Brazil twice before. I wanted to ask her advice on what to watch out for and for any hints and tips on what to do and not to do out there. We had a very interesting discussion hearing about her memories of her visits and meeting John of God. As we finished, she then said out of the blue, "It's okay to book your holiday now."

I had gentleman friend who was very spiritual and when he was enquiring as to when I was going to Brazil I replied, "I'm going in February for two weeks." He quickly replied, "But what if they want you to stay longer?" Longer? I had not thought of going anywhere longer than two weeks, I thought gosh I'm going to have to ask the Psychic Surgeons for guidance with this. So later that afternoon I connected to the Psychic Surgeons and asked them "Do you wish me to travel to Brazil for two weeks?" *"No."* Do you wish me to travel to Brazil for three weeks?" *"No."* "Do you wish me to travel to Brazil for four weeks?" *"Yes."* FOUR weeks? For four weeks! I've never been anywhere for four weeks. I had to quickly rethink my plans and check diary dates for my departure and return.

In the meantime, I had been informed that each time you make a visit The Casa and are presented to John of God you should be wearing 'all white' clothes. A mean feat to purchase white clothes in the middle of January but there were some sales on in the shops and I was able to buy what I needed.

The day of my spiritual journey arrived, the 4th of February 2018. I was being driven to Heathrow airport where I was to stay overnight due to the early morning flight departure. At the reception desk I was given my room key no 2211. Wow! Straightaway I thought two master numbers for my room? How interesting. Many more synchronicities were to follow:

The seat number on my flight to Portugal no 22.

My seat number on my connecting flight to Brazil no 22.

Above my seat on the cabin wall a small black triangle above my head. The male passenger beside me was called Bruno from Lyon in France and he was visiting, yes, you've guessed it, John of God! He even remarked in his broken English, "Out of three hundred passengers on this flight and we are sitting together doing the same trip!" Yes.

I was collected from the Brazil airport by my guide Robert and arrived that evening to my villa at the UK time of 22:11(pm.)

I smiled, and in my mind said, "Thank you Spirit."

As I had repeatedly seen the combination of numbers 2211, I went onto the internet and looked up the meaning of the Angel numbers 2211 and this was the explanation below:

"Angel numbers 2211 tells you to look upon new experiences and opportunities with optimism as they will bring about positive effects and favourable results, you are on a positive life path and are going in the right direction so have faith that wonderful opportunities will lead to happiness and personal fulfilment for you." Well that couldn't be more accurate could it?

Having taken a journal note pad with me to Brazil I knew that every day I had to capture and record all that was happening to me on this incredible journey. I know as you continue to read my account of this amazing spiritual journey you will be so surprised.

The villa I was staying in was impressive with its own grounds and only a fifteen-minute walk from The Casa Healing Centre. The villa belonged to my guide Robert, and there was a young couple already staying there from Canada. This was great as they were able to show me around having been there a week before me. My food and accommodation were included in the package Robert put together and in addition Robert was translating from Portuguese to English for me, as John of God only speaks Portuguese. Another perk of hiring Robert's services were that he was going to be guiding me to the shortest queues at The Casa Healing Centre as some of them were hours long.

In the afternoon of my first day after unpacking, Robert took me to The Casa to show me around and to get my bearings. It was much bigger than I had imagined. There were some lovely gardens full of exotic flowers and trees that were used for contemplation and meditation and of course for sitting in as the weather was gorgeous at 30c every day. In addition to the gardens there was a Reception, a Pharmacy, a Book store, a Café, a Water kiosk, brand new Toilets (courtesy of a gift from Oprah Winfrey) The Great Hall, The Current Room, The Blessings Room, The Healing Triangles, a Chapel, a Viewing platform, Crystal beds, there was a Soup kitchen, a Donations box and finally the car park.

There was a 5pm introduction meeting at The Casa that day that informed a large group of us of the procedures to follow for the next day, as in, which 'line' we had to stand in. We were instructed to go to the Book shop that was within The Casa grounds and collect a ticket for what was called the 'First Time Line' (this is the line to queue in when you have never seen John of God before.) It gets more complicated, but I will cover each 'line' description as and when I used them.

Also, in preparation for my first meeting with John of God and his Entities it was suggested that apart from wearing white clothing, I write a short list of what it is I would like the healing for. So, that evening I sat down and wrote a short list of five things I would like the healing to help me with.

Robert came to collect me at 8.20am the next day, he drove me to The Casa which was absolutely heaving with people. He took me through the staff entrance which took us through to the Great Hall to avoid the massive crowds of people all standing in line.

There were hundreds of people waiting in queues, some of whom had been there since 6.30am that morning. Robert and I only had to wait about 5-6 minutes and then we were ushered into the line (yes, I was queue jumping) but this is where being with a guide like Robert had its benefits and was all part of the service. The queue moved very slowly through into another room. This room was called the Current Room, silent, with many people dressed in white, sitting in rows on benches, meditating and holding the energy for the Medium John of God and his Entities to do the healing. Some people even had eye masks on to cover their eyes. This was a dedicated practice as I was later to find out, where sitting in 'Current' could often take as long as 3-4 hours of meditating! A session of meditation would not finish until all the people had been seen each morning and then again in the afternoons.

Along the walls and on the window blinds were many images of the Entities who carry the healing at The Casa. (Although these are called Entities in Brazil, they are spirit Psychic Surgeons, just like my own Team of Psychic Surgeons.) The main picture being that of Dom Inácio De Loyola who was the first Spirit Entity to connect with John of God and after whom John of God named the healing centre, Casa De Dom Inácio.

The queue moved along at a slow pace Robert was stood beside me as he needed to be there to translate any conversation to John of God. Whilst in the queue I had connected to the Psychic Surgeons I wanted them to share this experience with me. They were in my hands as we continued in line. I was so excited.

The weaving path of the queue turned a sharp left, and peering over the heads of others, I could see up ahead at the end of the room John of God sitting on his elevated throne like chair. Either side of the walkway there were enormous crystals at least 2 or 3 feet high leading up to where he was sitting.
Rose quartz, clear quartz, some of the crystals were globe shaped others were beautiful crystal columns. The whole of The Casa had been built on a bedrock of crystals, so the energy emanating from them was extremely powerful. There was also a statue of Saint Rita who is very important in Brazil. Either side of the walkway in between the crystals were twelve large wooden carved meditation chairs, six on one side and six on the other. There were twelve Mediums seated in these chairs all holding the energy for the healing.

We continued slowly in line until it was finally my turn. I could feel butterflies in my tummy, I was here at last, in front of this incredible man. John of God took hold of my right hand, and looked into my eyes, he was in his trance state where one of his Entities had taken over his body, so his blue eyes were cold and unblinking. Robert took from me my healing request list and spoke to him in Portuguese and John of God replied. He moved my hand to the right of him indicating I should now move along.
Robert said, "You now need to sit here," pointing to rows and rows of benches that were filling up with other people directed to sit in this area. This was the 'Entities Current Room', where the connection to the Spirit Entities starts to take place.

Robert said, "This is a special place you sit here with your eyes closed for maybe one or two hours until you are directed to leave." I chose a bench nearest to the wall; it was the second row from the front, and I could clearly see John of God from where I was sitting. I wanted to watch and observe him just as the Psychic Surgeons had said to do. But immediately one of the male room monitors spotted me and I was told to close my eyes.

As I sat down on the bench, I put my hands together in prayer position the Psychic Surgeons were still there in my hands, they acknowledged me fondly. Almost immediately a wave of emotion came over me and tears streamed down my cheeks, I knew it was releasing.

The Psychic Surgeons were in my hands moving and clearing the energy that no longer served me and preparing me for that afternoon's 'surgery' from the Entities. There was a lot of releasing from each of my chakras especially my heart chakra and my higher heart chakra. Another wave of emotion came over me with tears streaming down my face, this time I needed a tissue. Again, the Psychic Surgeons were moving my hands around me and over me, moving and using the wonderful energy. I asked them "How many Psychic Surgeons are around me?" And with my index finger they tapped six times. So, there were six Entities and Psychic Surgeons around me, helping me, clearing me, healing me, it was beautiful.

I could hear the voice of John of God clearly and opened my eyes to see that there was no one else left in the queue. Instead I could see three of his helpers passing to John of God a basket which contained many, many photographs and messages. These had been taken from the three wooden triangles situated around The Casa grounds, where people leave a photograph or a message asking the Entities for healing. Now John of God was moving his hands over the basket as his Entities gave the healing energy to the many requests for help. Again, I was caught looking by one of the room monitors and asked to close my eyes, which I did.

The Psychic Surgeons were still busy moving my hands using the energy, I wondered just how much extra healing they would be able to achieve because of the wonderfully strong energies at The Casa. As I sat there feeling emotional but beautifully calm suddenly in my mind's eye, I could see John of God! (Not in real life but in my mind.) He was smiling at me, he came forward and embraced me, he remained there for a few seconds and then he was gone.

Suddenly to break the silence I could hear a lady's voice speaking Portuguese, it sounded like she was saying the Lord's prayer, so I joined in, in English. After the prayer had finished, we were asked to leave. The room monitors were handing out small thimble sized cups of water blessed by the Entities to be given to each person after their connection to them.

As we came out of the room we were asked to turn right and head towards the Soup line. The sunshine was extremely bright having been inside with my eyes closed for nearly three hours.
I looked but couldn't see Robert, so I did as I was requested, and queued for my bowl of vegetable and pasta soup. I found a long bench table under the shade to sit with many other people who had just come from the same room. We excitedly exchanged comments about what had happened to each of us and how it felt. Robert found me and joined us around the table. Apparently, the soup is all part of the healing process and is given for free at The Casa for whoever needs it and every day there are hundreds of people that do.

When we had finished eating, I asked Robert if we could go to the viewing platform in the Gardens of Meditation. I wanted to see the views of Brazil that stretched out for miles across the valley to see the lush green trees that were in bloom and the varied vegetation. All of these were so exotic compared to our English countryside.

You could hear the call of many different birds, some parakeets, some macaws and there were hummingbirds too! I had to pinch myself, was I really in Brazil so close to the Amazon jungle? It was a lot to take in.

I asked Robert where in The Casa grounds were the healing triangles? As I wanted to put a list of names within the triangle to request healing from the Entities. We made our way to the nearest wall mounted triangle, I had to wait my turn until the lady in front of me had finished.

Then I placed the list of names on the bottom edge of the triangle and then placed my hands either side of it and I said a prayer. When I had finished my arms seemed to be taken over and on their own, (without my effort) were stretched out to the sides of me, in a cross formation and a wave of emotion came over me, my eyes filled with tears as I heard the words, *"Ask and it shall be given."* Now I do not usually hear words from Spirit in my head, so this was an extremely magical experience for me. No wonder I was crying. Once I had finished at the triangle, I met up with Robert again, he had been watching me and said, "You are a sensitive." (I know).

That afternoon, Robert informed me we would be returning at 2pm to The Casa, where I was to have my 'surgery.' He said, "We will be going to The Passa Room where the surgery will take place and then when it is finished, we will return you to the villa where it is 24 hours of complete bed rest for you." Just before 2pm Robert collected me and drove me to The Casa.

Just as before we were ushered into the queue to make our way in line through to the Current Room. John of God was not there sitting in his chair, instead I was ushered by the room monitors to sit on one of the benches. I chose to sit at the end of the bench by the walkway (to give me more room) as I knew the Psychic Surgeons would be coming forward into my hands again. We were told to close our eyes as 'surgery' was about to begin. I sat there for thirty minutes. As I had hoped, the Psychic Surgeons came forward and into my hands. I had no tears this time and the Psychic Surgeons used my hands and formed a triangle with my fingers, this they did many times during the thirty minute session. At the end of the session we were told to open our eyes and there standing in front of us, was John of God. He said a prayer in Portuguese and then it was time to leave.

We all filed out of the room into the bright sunshine and were handed a prescription and told to go to the English-speaking monitor who would inform us of what we 'can and cannot' do for the next 24 hours after surgery.

We were told first and foremost; we must have complete bedrest. To stay in our room for 24 hours. (What?) We can get out of bed to use the toilet facilities and for mealtimes only and then to return to bed. There can be:

No reading, no writing, no use of mobile phone, no internet, no TV, no music, no spicy foods, no drinking alcohol, no sitting in direct sunshine, no exercise for eight days and finally no sex for forty days. So, basically, I was to do nothing at all for the next 24 hours!

We were told you will need to drink only the 'blessed water' for twelve days after surgery. Stitches will be removed after seven days, (stitches, what stitches?) this will be done during the night on the seventh day, and you will need to wear something white that night. Goodness me, I wasn't expecting that!

Plus, we had to take the herb tablets we were to purchase with our prescription from the Pharmacy at The Casa and take them every day for the next forty days!

Robert took the prescription from me and went to the Casa Pharmacy where he purchased the container of 80 herb tablets. One tablet twice a day. They weren't cheap I think it worked out to about £15 per container, so although the beautiful healing was free the herb tablets were not. Robert drove me back to the villa and by 3pm that afternoon I was confined to bed for 24 hours.

I slept a lot at first, the herb tablets contain a sedative so probably why I felt drowsy and of course the after effects of the healing from the Entities. The Psychic Surgeons were in my hands and moved them from my midriff to my abdomen, then to my head, to my chest and then to my lower back. I was so pleased they were with me.

I could see from my bed through the window that the night was drawing in, there had been a thunderstorm with heavy rain whilst I had been asleep. My meals were brought to me on a tray, I was to leave the tray outside of my bedroom door and then go back to bed. During that night I could feel the Entities working on me. At one point my hand was placed over my higher heart chakra and I asked, "Are you giving healing to my Soul?" *"Yes."* On waking the next morning at 7.30am I received fresh fruit for my breakfast. My back was aching after being laid on the bed for so long, so I asked the Psychic Surgeons if I could have some healing to relieve it please and this they did for me.

The sunshine was streaming through the window now and I knew this was going to be the longest part of the day as I still had six hours to endure just lying on my bed, from 9am through to 3pm in the afternoon. I had taken another herb tablet with my blessed water and before long I was asleep. Again, the Psychic Surgeons were in my hands performing healing on me. At one point I asked, "Are the John of God Entities still working on me?" *"Yes."*

I awoke at 2pm and was relieved to see on the clock that I only had one hour left before I could get up. But I was fidgety, I had slept all that I could, and my back was aching again from laying down for so long. I asked, "Can I get up yet?" *"No wait until 3pm."* Almost to the minute of 3pm I got up out of bed and freshened up, cleaned my teeth, brushed my hair and was starting to feel like me again. A light snack for lunch and then I made my way, quite slowly, which surprised me, out into the garden and the fresh air. I sat in the shade on the balcony overlooking the villa garden admiring the view. Having had so much rest I thought I would be full of beans, but really, I felt quite the opposite, lethargic and with no energy. I was pleased to be able to do things again, like reading and using my phone, but everything was done in slow motion and by 10.30pm that night I was ready for bed. Unbelievable! I linked in with the Psychic Surgeons, and they confirmed that no further healing was required now just rest, but they did cleanse and clear me from the days' limited activities.

This was now day three of my visit to Brazil and it turned out to be one of 'the most' amazing days of my life! Anyone who had received the 'surgery' from John of God and the Entities had to follow up the healing received with an afternoon visit of sitting in The Current Room at The Casa. This was to meditate and send unconditional love and healing energy for John of God to use.

This was so he and the Entities could give healing to the many people who were arriving at The Casa that day.

Robert collected me at 1pm to take me to The Casa. I was pleased that he was driving me to The Casa as I still felt a little delicate from the surgery I had received. The afternoon session did not start until 2pm so the people who had arrived early like myself, were chatting to each other. I then noticed a lady sitting on one of the benches to the left of me, it was the lady from Glastonbury! She was here, at The Casa, at the same time as my own visit! I was able to catch her eye, we waved to each other.

We said we would meet up later. I found my seat on one of the wooden benches at the front of the room and from where I was sitting I was able to see John of God's chair so that I might at some point be able to observe him during the afternoon. We had been directed that once seated we were to close our eyes at 1.30pm to start to raise the vibration to help and assist John of God. Quite a few people had brought a cushion to sit on as the benches were wooden with no padding, and I was to experience the discomfort of a numb bottom later that afternoon, because I had no cushion.

I sat very quietly, cleared my mind and sent out the healing vibrations, I felt the Angels around me as I did so, a really beautiful energy. Quite some time had passed, I was very relaxed, my mind full of the beautiful healing vibrations that surrounded me from all the other people in the Current Room.

As I sat and concentrated, I suddenly felt a very firm presence push forward into my body. A really peculiar feeling, like I couldn't breathe properly, like my lungs were being squashed, it felt laboured to breathe. This was very strange, I'd never felt anything like this before, even the Psychic Surgeons do not do this to me!

My hands were moved into the prayer position, as if the Psychic Surgeons had joined me. I was not expecting them to do so as it would have interfered with my meditations and concentration during the session.

81

I asked, "Is this the Psychic Surgeons?" "No" was the reply. (Well who could it be, I thought?)

"Is this one of John of God's Entities?" "Yes." (OMG!)

I said, "Greetings to you today and thank you for coming forward." I was able to communicate with the Entity through my hand actions, just as I do with the Psychic Surgeons, but still only receiving a yes or no reply to my questions.

What an incredible experience I thought, I have one of John of God's Entities here within me, within my own body, and he didn't even ask permission.

I thought I must ask him some questions, so I asked,

"Was he here with me to give me some healing?" "No."

"Was he here to feel my energy?" "Yes."

"Are we to work together?" "Yes." (How exciting).

"Together, here in Brazil?" "Yes."

"Also, back in the UK?" "No."

"Does John of God know you are here with me?" "Yes."

"Does he need some healing?" "Yes."

"Is now an appropriate time?" "Yes."

I started to channel the Universal white light and, in my mind, placed John of God in a light filled pyramid, the Entity liked this. I asked him,

"Am I doing this correctly for you?" "Yes."

"Can John of God feel this healing for him?" "Yes." Then I asked the Entity,

"Have I seen your portrait around The Casa?" "Yes."

"Are you the Entity by the Healing triangle?" "Yes."

In my minds' eye I could see an image of a gentleman with piercing blue eyes and a beard, I was sure this was the Entity who had connected with me today. In my mind I said to him that I would look out for his portrait and take a photograph of him to keep.

As the afternoon progressed the Entity remained with me, from time to time he would move my hands from the restful pose of, hands on my lap, to moving my hands in two circles which made the infinity sign. I asked him,

"Is this sign my link with the Psychic Surgeons?" "Yes."

"Is it the link with the healing?" "Yes."

"Will you stay with me for the duration of Current?" "Yes."

By now, at least one and a half hours had passed, and my bottom was getting numb on the hard-wooden bench. (Where was a cushion when I needed one?) I was fidgety and was even considering getting up to leave.

We had been told that we could leave but that we would not be allowed to return in that session. My left knee wanted to be stretched out so that the kneecap could click and be comfortable again. I asked the Entity "Would he be able to give some healing to my left knee please?" "Yes." The Entity started to move my hands, my left hand cupped my left kneecap, whilst the fingers of my right hand pointed like lasers to the kneecap, then after a little while my right hand was moved and pointed to my groin. Then my left hand was moved to my left hip where it remained for a few minutes, then both hands were returned to the prayer position. The Entity was showing me he had finished.

I thanked him and then jokingly in my mind said, "Could you give me healing on my bottom please as it has gone numb from sitting on the wooden bench?" "Yes." With that, each buttock was lifted and squeezed as if returning the blood to them. (I'm now smiling, if only the people around me knew what was happening!) This action was repeated several times until I felt like I was sitting on a cushion! I was so grateful. I thanked him so much and told him I would now stay for the duration of the session.

I asked him,

"Am I going to be working with John of God?" "No."

"Am I to return to Brazil again?" "Yes."

"More than once?" "Yes." In my head came the words "many times."

"And you would work through me in Brazil?" "Yes."

"Are you enjoying being in my energy?" "Yes."

After another half an hour had passed, I asked, "Are we nearly finished?" "No."

"Do we have one more hour yet?" "Yes."

I continued to sit quietly. There was no one else filing passed us to be received by John of God.

I asked, "Is it finished now?" "No."

I asked the Entity if he would stay with me when I left the Current Room, to give me enough time to walk to the Healing triangle, to what I believed was his portrait before he left my physical body, he said, "Yes." At the end of the session prayers were said over us and then we said the Lord's prayer and it was now time to go. I was given some blessed water on leaving the Current Room and quickly made my way to the wall mounted Healing triangle. And there on the opposite wall was the Entity's portrait. I asked, "Was he still with me?" "Yes."

I pointed with my finger, "Is this you?" "Yes."

I took two photographs of his portrait; so pleased I could finally see his image. I was still none the wiser as to who he might be. I then made my way out into the sunlight into the gardens.

It was so wet outside, there had been a thunder and lightning storm and torrential rain whilst I had been in the Current Room all afternoon. I returned to the Reception area as arranged to meet up again with my guide Robert. I could see him waiting for me in his car. I showed him the photograph I had taken of the Entity and asked him, "Who is this?" "Oh, replied Robert, he is the principle Entity at The Casa, he is the Chief Surgeon."

"His name is Dr Augusto Almedes." Wow the Chief Surgeon had come to me! It all made sense now especially as I am working with Surgeons too, the Psychic Surgeons. I felt so privileged to have been chosen by him that day.

(Entity Dr Augusto and the second picture of Entity Dom Inácio)

On returning to the villa I excitedly told the Canadian lady, Bronwen, what had happened that afternoon in the Current Room and showed her the photograph of the Entity, Dr Augusto that had linked with me. She agreed with me it was incredible and wanted to know more. That evening I sat on the veranda in the warmth of the evening and updated my journal. It felt strange recalling all that had happened to me because it felt as if the Entity was still with me. So, I asked,

"Are you still here?" "Yes."

"I know who you are, you are Dr Augusto, is that correct?" "Yes."

"Have you ever done this before with another channel?" "No."

"Can you see?" "No."

"Can you sense?" "Yes."

"Are you looking to work through another Medium?" "No."

"Could you also work through me?" "Yes."

I asked, "Have we finished now?" "Yes."

I thanked him for coming forward today and for the healing he gave me, as I felt fantastic! Dr Augusto acknowledged my communication through my hands, and I could feel his energy move away from my body, I could breathe much easier too. My hands then went into the prayer position and suddenly the Psychic Surgeons came into my hands, I thanked them for allowing the Entity, Dr Augusto, to 'use' me as his channel that afternoon. They seemed pleased. The Psychic Surgeons then cleansed and cleared me back into balance again after this incredible Entity connection. What an experience.

One week had passed of my Spiritual journey in Brazil and I was now to move accommodation from the large villa to the Hotel Raphael that was located in the main street and nearer to the Healing Centre, The Casa. The synchronicity of this hotel name did not pass me by, Raphael is the healing Archangel who works through me and here I was staying in his named hotel. The hotel was very nice, but was not as luxurious as the villa and it had no outdoor garden space to sit in. But this was a good thing because it allowed me to mix with more people than I had done previously at the villa. There were many hotel guests of different nationalities, many of whom had terrible debilitating conditions. As a healer myself all I wanted to do was help them, but I knew this was already in the hands of John of God and the Entities.

Our meals at the hotel were buffet style and we could sit at any dining table of our choice. Sometimes my guide Robert would join me for a meal, and he introduced me to other people that he knew, which was great. One lady he introduced me to was an American lady called Amanda. Petite and attractive in her early thirties she and I got on like a house on fire.
Amanda was with another guide's group and had been at the hotel visiting The Casa for the previous three weeks. She knew of all the best places to take me. (She laughs).

In the town of Abadiania where The Casa is situated there really is nothing to do! During the time period of healing that you receive at The Casa, no alcohol is permitted at all. There is no alcohol permitted in the town, so no pubs, clubs or bars to visit, not that I wanted to. There were quite a few crystal shops and a few coffee houses though, some restaurants and by far the most popular place to visit was Frutti's, a restaurant famous for its fruit smoothies, which were delicious.

There were cooked meals on the menu too. Amanda and I would meet up there most days to catch up on our days' activities. I was introduced by the Canadian couple from the villa to this place too and we had several meals at Frutti's together. There was also an evening of musical entertainment, which made a lovely change. As you can imagine it got very busy.

Another lady I met was from New York, she had been to The Casa three times previously for an ongoing health condition that was being treated by John of God and the Entities.

She was very interested in my own journey as a Psychic Surgeon and when I said I had a copy of my book with me she asked if she could borrow it to read. She then linked to spirit and said, "You will need to find a clinic like The Casa where people can come."

I thanked her for the message. She liked that I was a lady Psychic Surgeon, she said "We need more!" She said, "I have never seen such a pure channel as yours before, no wonder the Entities want to work through you!"

A few days later I decided to make a visit the Santa Rita chapel within The Casa grounds. A tiny little chapel which was only able to seat six people. On the wall was a picture of Saint Rita who I had never heard of before but who was extremely popular in Brazil. I had been told there were some very powerful energies in this chapel, and I wanted to take some time to sit there and meditate. No sooner had I sat down to make myself comfortable, when an 'Entity' entered my tummy again, just like before with the Entity Dr Augusto. I asked,
"Are you the same Entity as before?" "No."
"Have we linked together before?" "No."
"Was I to receive healing from you?" "Yes."

The Entity proceeded moved my hands, just as the Psychic Surgeons do, over my main chakra points and when he had finished my hands were returned to my lap. Still restricted in my breathing by the Entity, I tried to take a deep breath and could not, well that was certainly different. I sat quietly, as the Entity removed its energy from me, and I was trying to correct my breathing again. Then in the blink of an eye, as I sat there quietly, another of The Casa Entities entered my tummy. I said, "Greetings and thank you for coming forward" and then the Entity proceeded to perform more healing on me. When he had finished my hands were returned to my lap.

I asked, "Has Dr Augusto asked you to come forward to link with me today? "Yes."
"Are we to work together in the future?" "Yes."
"Have you finished now?" "Yes."

Thank goodness for that I thought. I quickly left the chapel before any further Entity visits and returned to my hotel for lunch. Afterwards went to my room to rest and sleep after the incredible healing I had received.

The next day I decided to go to the meditation gardens with the hope that I might be undisturbed by the Entities and actually get some meditation done. But no, that was not to be because who did I see in the gardens but the lady from Glastonbury! We had a lovely long catch up and I told her all that had been happening to me since arriving at The Casa. She listened intently and then said, "I'm not surprised." We promised to meet up again, but our paths never crossed.

The next day at 8.30am Robert had arranged to collect me from the hotel and take me to The Casa to join the 'Revision Line'. In this line, you have to queue to see John of God, for your condition to be reviewed by the Entities since having had their surgery. But on this day, The Casa was absolutely heaving with people, even more than usual. It was Ash Wednesday, and many Brazilian people came to The Casa for healing but also to repent any sins and to be cleansed by the Entities. We could hardly move! I suggested to my guide Robert that maybe it would be better (and a shorter queue) if we were to join Line 2 instead? Line 2 was classed as 'the Second Timers Line' for those who had already seen John of God before and were being assessed to possibly have another surgery. Robert thought this was a good idea and with his connections with the Casa staff, he was able to get me in line to see John of God much quicker.

The line moved quite quickly this day and soon it was my turn to stand in front of John of God for the second time. Again, he took my right hand, Robert spoke to him in Portuguese, and it was decided that I was in need of another 'surgery' that afternoon. We came out into the sunlight and it was still only 9.30am.

We looked around and there were still hundreds of people queueing to see John of God and he would see them all, each and every one of them. What we didn't know was how long it would take for him to see everyone!

The afternoon surgery sessions normally began at 2pm, but my guide Robert found out that the morning session had only just finished, and that John of God needed to rest. Robert suggested we meet again at 3.45pm to get into the queue as the afternoon session would begin at 4pm.

This afternoon session was for me to have my second 'surgery'. As before, I had expected to be guided into the Passa Room to receive the surgery, but instead I was in the queue to see John of God again. Twice in one day! This time as I approached him there seemed to be a slight smile on his face. (I wondered if the Entity had recognised my energy.) Robert spoke to John of God in Portuguese, he then signalled for me to sit in the Entities Current Room to his right. The male room monitor directed me to sit on the end of the row on the bench.

Straight away a Casa Entity entered my body, not knowing who it could be, I asked,
"Have you come forward to be with me from before?" "Yes."
"Are you Dr Augusto?" "Yes."
"Are you going to give me healing today?" "Yes."
He then proceeded to move my hands scooping and taking away energy blockages from my sacral and base chakras and he repeated this several times.
When he had finished, he returned my hands into my lap. In my mind I said to Dr Augusto, "The room monitors would get such a shock if they knew what we were doing". "Yes" was his reply and then he cupped my face with my hands as if in agreement.
I asked, "Would he be giving me any guidance?" "Yes."

"Would this be in my sleep state?" "Yes."

"Will I remember it?" "No." (not at the moment).

"Did you introduce your other Team Entities to me the other day in the chapel?" "Yes."

"Will they be working with me also?" "Yes."

I then asked Dr Augusto,

"Have you ever worked through anyone else other than John of God?" "No."

Then suddenly I heard a man's voice speaking the Lord's prayer and the healing session was nearly over. I asked Dr Augusto,

"Do I need surgery?" "No."

"Do I need to come to the Current Room tomorrow afternoon?" "Yes."

We were asked to get up and leave and I was handed the blessed water, I thanked the room monitor for his kindness. I made my way to the Great Hall which was much quieter now there were no queues as most people had been seen by John of God.

I had noticed on the side wall of the Great Hall a video playing; it was showing John of God being filmed whilst carrying out his 'physical' surgeries, which he was famous for. I decided to sit down and watch this very carefully, as up until now I had not seen or heard of any physical surgeries taking place whilst I had been at The Casa. The video was showing where the Entities were actually using metal instruments via John of God's hands to carry out the surgery. John of God was scraping a lady's eyeball with what looked like a kitchen knife on her right eye!

There was some blood and tears, but no skin was being removed. I had seen many videos on the internet of John of God's Entities inserting instruments up into the nose of the patient and removing tumours growths and cysts. I wondered if I would get to see a 'physical' surgery in the remaining time I was there. Did I really want to see a physical surgery whilst I was there? I was in two minds.

I went back to my hotel room to rest before later meeting up with my guide Robert for dinner. He informed me that I was to have surgery the following morning, this I found a little confusing as Dr Augusto had said I did not need any. But then what do I know! Robert said we were to meet at The Casa at 8am.

Robert and I met up at The Casa the next morning and we stood in the queue of the 'Second Time Line.' In the Current Room there were many people who had already been there since 7am sending and building up the healing energies to the Entities for the healing. As the queue continued I noticed John of God was not in his chair, but as I got nearer, I was handed another prescription which I gave to Robert. I was directed to sit in the Entities Current Room for thirty minutes. On this occasion there were no Entity interruptions. When I came out into the sunshine Robert had been to the Pharmacy to get my prescription filled with more herbs. As this was the second surgery I had received, more herbs were needed to be taken, I was to start taking this next batch of herbs only after I had finished the first. That meant I would be taking these herbs home with me back to the UK as it was another forty-day supply.

By 8.45am that morning I was back in my hotel room for my 24-hour confinement. The hotel Reception staff had been notified by Robert that I was to receive each of my 3 meals on a tray to my room. I in turn had to leave the tray outside my room when I had finished and then return to bed. So, I lay there, I knew exactly what was coming, a day in bed which actually felt as long as a week!
Outside of my room I could hear in the corridor people leaving their room to go out for the day. From my bedroom window I could see it was a sunny day and oh how I missed being outside.
I had taken another herb tablet and soon I was dropping off to sleep, but this was only for a couple of hours, I had already had a full night's sleep the night before. As I lay there, thoughts came into my mind. I really want to write them down, but I can't. I asked my main spirit guide, "Can I read?" "No."

I slept some more and then there was a gentle knock at the door, the hotel staff were bringing me my lunch tray. Hooray at last something to do! Lunch was delicious I savoured every mouthful and took my time eating it because once I had finished it was the dreaded hours of 'nothing'. But fortunately, after I returned my tray back out into the corridor, I settled myself down and fell asleep all afternoon. Then at 6pm the hotel staff brought my evening dinner tray, a bit earlier than my usual dinnertime, but again a welcome interruption. I could hear people coming and going in the corridor outside of my room. I wondered where they were going, I wished I could be going with them.

I called the Psychic Surgeons into my hands and I asked them,
"Is everything going according to plan?" "Yes."
"Is my healing progressing well?" "Yes."
"Do you need to do anything to help me this evening?" "No."
"Should I settle down and go to sleep?" "Yes."

Well that's easier said than done. By 9pm only twelve hours had passed of my twenty four hour confinement, and I only had another twelve hours to get through. You cannot believe how long and drawn out twelve hours can be, when you are allowed to do nothing, nothing at all! After my evening meal I took another herb tablet and yes, sleep finally came. I was woken up the following morning by a knocking on my bedroom door, it was the hotel staff bringing me my breakfast at 6am! 6am is that all?
That really was early, but I'm glad they remembered and brought my breakfast to me. By the time I had finished it was 7am and I only had one and a half hours left of my confinement. I called the Psychic Surgeons through to my hands, they confirmed there was nothing to do but to wait for 8.30am when I would be able to get up and shower and get ready to get out into the sunshine and fresh air. Yippee!

That day I met up with my friend and we sat and chatted the whole afternoon, she introduced me to her friend Michael. A man from Germany who had been at The Casa for three months. He was very interested to learn all about my healing and the Psychic Surgeons, and we arranged to meet up another time.

I had been at the San Raphael Hotel for one week and it was now time to leave and move into my final accommodation the 'pink coloured villa' for the last two weeks of my stay. Robert helped me move my luggage from the hotel into the new smaller villa and then he took me food shopping as I now had to cook my own meals there. Once we returned to the pink villa, he left me to sort myself out, unpacking the food into the kitchen cupboards and also unpacking and hanging up my clothes, again! The two bedroomed villa was lovely and clean, there was a comfortable living room area, two ensuite bedrooms, the kitchen come dining room and a small garden at the front of the property where I could sit out. One day whilst doing just that I saw a hummingbird at my kitchen window, it darted back and forth maybe catching flies from the fly screen covering the villa window. He was too quick for me to take a photograph of him, but what a delight to see a hummingbird so close up.

I had arranged to meet up with the lady from New York and Michael at 12.30 in preparation to join them as we were all going to the Current Meditation Room for the afternoon.
She had other friends with her and got separated from myself and Michael. So we two made our way into the Current Room, chose a bench to sit on with a view, and yes, I had a comfy cushion to sit on this time. I had a good view of John of God at the far end of the room, and from time to time opened my right eye only to observe him. I kept my left eye closed so that the room monitors would not notice me looking around. (She smiles).

94

Almost as soon as I was seated a Casa Entity came forward and entered into my body again taking my breath away as he did so. He indicated that I was receiving healing whilst I sat there.

My hand movements were more discrete this time, but Michael felt the movements of my arm and smiled, because he knew what was happening.

We met up with friends afterwards and made our way to Frutti's for a smoothie and told them what had happened during the meditation session. It was time to return to my villa for the evening and Michael and I seemed to be walking in the same direction, it turned out that his accommodation was exactly opposite mine. This enabled him to escort me safely to my villa which I was very grateful for. I'm guessing that Spirit had put this into place to make sure I was safe.

Michael and I arranged to meet first thing at The Casa café to have a coffee and a catch up and he informed me that he had found a small pink plastic key, there were numbers on the key itself and when added together made the number 22. (Oh, I thought the number is back again.) We thought that this could be a synchronicity for the day, and we were both to keep our eyes peeled for any event.

Today was 'Revision Line' day and having had my second surgery I needed to be reviewed again. Michael stood behind me in the queue, sure that something was going to happen today.

We are told that Dr Augusto is in Entity within John of God today, so in my mind I wondered if there would be any recognition from him when I reached John of God to be reviewed. Then suddenly, in the queue up ahead of us there was a commotion, there was a child, he had collapsed, John of God called for a chair and for his instruments and then started to perform 'physical surgery' on the child. We were too far away to see exactly what was being done but watched to see the child with his Mother being wheeled out of the room.

95

Everything returned to normal, the queue continued moving towards John of God. As I approached getting nearer and nearer to him, I asked a female interpreter if she would be kind enough to help me, as my guide Robert was not with me that day to interpret. This was just in case there were any words spoken in Portuguese from John of God. I needed not to have worried, no words were spoken as he and his Entity Dr Augusto looked into my eyes and took my hand, then guided me to sit on the benches to his right, as I had done before.

Behind me, Michael was in conversation with John of God, and he was being told, "You are healed, you can go home now." Michael is thrilled but also confused as his physical condition was not yet completely corrected. We agreed we would speak about it at length once we had finished in the Entity's Current Room. We took our seats on the bench and sat quietly. Straight away a Casa Entity came forward into my body, but more gently so that I did not have to gasp for breath. This was becoming a habit! I asked,
"If the Entity had been to me before?" "Yes" In my mind I got the word DOM.
"Was I receiving healing?" "Yes."
After we had finished in the Current Room and had a drink of blessed water, Michael spoke to his own German guide about what had happened with John of God, and she explained it so that he had a full understanding of what had happened.

I felt Michael would not go home immediately to Germany but may be become a volunteer at The Casa to help others and he would be free to sit in the Current Room whenever he wanted to and still receive the healing he felt he needed. He seemed very happy with this suggestion.

Michael and I made our way to the Meditation gardens where we sat on one of the benches in the dappled shade enjoying the view and talking quietly so as not to disturb others.

I said to Michael "Who is DOM?" He replied, "Why do you ask?" I said, "Because that's who came to me this afternoon in the Entity Current Room". Michael then almost screeched out loud his reply to me, "That's Dom Inácio!". "You had Dom Inácio come to you today?" "Yes" I replied a bit bewildered, "Why?"

He replied, "He is the Entity that The Casa is named after, Paula that is incredible!" "I know". And of course, there was a reason for this introduction with Dom, and all would become clear a few days later.

Later that evening I connected to my spirit guide and asked, "Would there be an opportunity in my last week here to see or meet John of God?" The reply was, "Yes next Friday, I am to give him healing." Well that was an exciting reply, I wondered just how that was going to happen?

The next morning, I decided it was time to get some sun to my skin and do some sunbathing. I didn't want to return home to the UK looking as pale as when I had left. But the sun was so hot, each day the temperature was around 33c. So, I put on my suntan lotion and sunbathed early morning until 12 noon only, when it got just too hot to be out in it. It was a good routine because I was resting, reading my book and then going to The Casa for the afternoon to attend the Current Room meditation.

On this, the last Wednesday afternoon of my stay I was on my way to The Casa, when I bumped into Michael. We made our way to the Meditation gardens to catch up on all our news as we had not seen each other for a few days. I told him of my horror when a Gecko lizard ran very quickly across the kitchen work surface and then proceeded to climb up the wall into the kitchen wall cupboard, which I never used again, we laughed.

We made our way to the Current Room queue and as we filed into the empty room, we chose our bench to sit on, but always in view of John of God's chair. I had my cushion to sit on and my blessed water to drink during the very long session. Then saying "Hello" to quite a few people I knew by sight before we were instructed to begin the meditation and raising the healing vibrations for John of God and the Entities.

I found this so peaceful, my mind was calm and then suddenly, I could feel a Casa Entity enter my body. Today, it was a very strong pulling feeling in my tummy and straight away I asked,

"Is that DOM?" "No."

"Is that Dr Augusto?" "Yes."

I smiled and in my mind thanked him for coming forward, this must have been at least his third time of connecting with me in this way, and as I sat quietly so he began to give me healing, concentrating on my abdomen, moving my own hands very discretely. I asked,

"After today do I need any more healing?" "No."

"Is he pleased with how my healing has progressed?" "Yes."

"Do I return to the Revision Line on Thursday morning?" "Yes."

"Will my own healing have changed when I go back to the UK?" "Yes."

"Will I have an opportunity to meet John of God?" "Yes."

"On Thursday?" "No."

"On Friday after the Goodbye Line?" "Yes."

"Will I be giving him healing?" "Yes."

"Is this part of my mission to come to Brazil?" "Yes."

I am quiet now, no more questions but in my mind is processing the information he had given me. Dr Augusto continued working on my abdomen, my heart chakra and throat chakra. Every time I thought of John of God, Dr Augusto sensed this and placed my hands around my face, I knew he was pleased.

Michael was sitting to my right with an eye pad over his eyes, I asked Dr Augusto,

"Is Michael healed?" "Yes."
"Will he volunteer at The Casa?" "No."
"Will he help people in other ways?" "Yes."
I thanked him for his guidance and would pass this information onto Michael later. Dr Augusto remained within me for the rest of the meditation session.

I decided to open my eyes to see if I could see John of God, just as he was walking past me. He stopped at two ladies seated on benches in front of me and then continued until he reached his throne like chair. He began to receive the people waiting in line for the healing. Some were able bodied and walking, some were in wheelchairs, others were limping as they walked, and some people were assisted by their own carer. Many people however disabled they were, would attempt to bend down on one knee in front of John of God and kiss his left hand, this left some people unable to get up again and they had to be assisted, there was so much love for this incredible man, who had devoted over fifty-five years of his life to the healing of others.
Now in his late seventies he still kept to the routine of healing at The Casa three days a week, Wednesdays, Thursdays and Fridays.

Finally, a lady began to say a prayer over us, and we joined in with the Lord's prayer, we were then given the blessed water and left the Current Room to walk out into the fresh air. Michael and I decided to go to The Casa café for a coffee and vegan cake and he insisted on paying, I said to him that I had a message for him from Dr Augusto and explained that the Chief Surgeon had come forward to me in the Current Room, I relayed to him the message that had been given to me.

Michael said, "Thank you so much, I will miss you when you go home on Saturday." I thanked him and I told him I was ready to return to the UK now.

We arranged to meet up Thursday morning. I had been told by Dr Augusto to queue in the Revision Line for 9.30am. I hoped I would be given the 'all clear' as I was due to return home on Saturday. Michael didn't need to attend the Revision Line, but he queued with me anyway to keep me company. Just as I had hoped I received the 'all clear' from John of God, and as I looked into his eyes, I wondered if he knew we were going to give him healing.

I was guided to go and sit in the Blessings Room to give thanks and to sit there for thirty minutes. Whilst sitting there quietly, one of The Casa Entities gently came forward into my body. I asked,

"Is this Dom Inácio?" "Yes." I thanked him for coming forward today, I asked,

"Will I get the chance to see John of God tomorrow (Friday?)" "Yes."

"After I have been in the Goodbye Line?" "Yes."

"Will I be able to give him some healing?" "Yes."

So, I had been guided twice now that 'somehow' I was to link with John of God to give him some healing. It made me nervous, how was this going to happen? I just had to trust.

That afternoon in the Casa Meditation gardens I asked Michael if he would be kind enough to take some photographs of me in the gardens as a keep sake of my time there at The Casa.

I showed him how to use the camera on my mobile phone and in my white outfit, he managed to take some lovely shots. I thought it would be lovely to use these photographs for my website on my return to the UK.

These are some of the photographs taken.

That evening on the internet I chatted to some friends in the UK on my social media page and listened to everyone's struggle with the deep snow, this was the storm called 'The Beast from the East' and it had brought the country to a standstill. I just hoped that I would still be able to land in the UK when I returned home in two days' time.

Whilst on my social media page I connected to a dear friend, she knew I was in Brazil and asked if I was having an amazing time, she then said, "I have a message for you". She then proceeded to channel the following message to me from The Divine Angels at The Casa.

From the Divine Angels of this sacred place in Brazil. They said to me,

"Beloved one we are the Angels who have been working with you whilst you are staying here in Brazil and the visits of healing that you are achieving with this divine person (John of God)."

"We are the Angels and Healers who are present and who work with this divine person, who you are currently visiting."

"We come forward with a message of love for you."
"So much is being achieved within your being while you are on this sacred journey that you have decided on a Soul level to take."
"We have been working through your Akashic records, currently helping to clear away any obstacles that are no longer needed and are hindering your current healing work that you do in the UK. Because it is time for your business to grow."
"It's time to take your business to other countries and this you will be doing very well indeed. This was the experience Paula for you to realise more fully, the Healer that you are growing into."
"Not only is it for your own personal healing but it's also an Awakening that when you come back to the UK this will be realised. It may take you Paula quite a while to fully come back into your body."
"For example what we mean here, is that even though physically you will be back in the UK at home, energetically and spiritually you will still travel and continue to receive healing within this divine place for as long as you need it. So, understand the healing is not just on a physical level here, but the work you are doing with this divine person and with ourselves is on a much bigger scale than you currently understand."
"Our message to you was to let you know what IS actually happening for you now. We are preparing your healing channel for the international work as the Healer you will grow into, in the near future."
"Know that all is well, all is progressing beautifully and abundantly for you. An amazing journey for you".
"We are the Divine Healing Angels of this sacred place in Brazil".

I was completely blown away by this message. How absolutely beautiful, that The Angels would come forward to give me this message, I really felt quite emotional. I thanked my friend for channeling the message to me and promised we would connect again on my return.

Friday arrived, my last full day at the pink coloured villa, it was a leisurely day as I did not need to be at The Casa until 4pm that afternoon to join the 'Goodbye Line' and give my thanks personally to John of God for the healing he had given to me over the previous four weeks. I packed my suitcase and was ready for my journey home to the UK. I had received a message that the snow there had been cleared and I would be able to safely return. I sat in the villa garden for the last time enjoying the warmth of the sun on my skin, knowing that when I returned to the UK it was going to be freezing cold!

That afternoon I made my way to The Casa and met Michael there, not sure of where to go, we asked one of the helpers, "Where do we queue for the 'Goodbye Line' please?" "Oh, it's finished early today, it is finished." Finished I thought, how can that be?
I had been guided to arrive at The Casa for 4pm, and here we were at 4pm and the line was finished. Michael could see I was tearful, how was I going to help John of God now? Then I remembered that there was on a Friday afternoon a photo opportunity to have your picture taken with John of God, well maybe this was where the connection was to take place. Michael and I made our way to The Casa Reception where a large group of about fifty people were waiting outside, I said to Michael, "This must be the right place."

Sure enough, within minutes John of God appeared and stood with groups of people to have his picture taken with them. Because I was on my own, we were not permitted to have individual photos taken with him.

So I was asked to stand on the end of a group of people (whom I didn't know) and wait for John of God to come over to us. To my delight I could see that John of God was making his way directly over to where I was standing. He positioned himself between me and the group I had been tagged onto. John of God was now standing to the right of me, and his left hand was down by his side, as quick as a flash, I slipped my right hand into his left hand and we held hands. OMG, this was it, this was the 'connection' that we needed to make! I was over the moon, I smiled, in fact I beamed with happiness.

Michael had my mobile phone ready to take 'the photo' of me with John of God, but he was struggling, something was wrong, he had turned my phone off by mistake. Oh no! The opportunity was lost to have a photo taken with John of God. Deeply disappointed, I managed to get my phone working again. I tried to get near to him, to take another photo but it was too late.

John of God ready for photos and then with a small group.
I managed to take some other photos of John of God as he stood with other groups, but I could not get another chance for a photo opportunity with him on my own.

My only consolation was that 'contact' had been made, how lucky was that? And this was all that Spirit had asked me to do. I nearly messed it up, but in the end, I had done what they had asked. I had achieved all that I had needed to do, or so I thought...

Michael and I decided that as it was my last evening, we should treat ourselves and go out for a pizza. Yes, I certainly know how to live the high life. It was our last evening of friendship and I was grateful to Michael for helping me during my stay. We reminisced over dinner about the last few weeks, on how our paths had crossed and what had happened to the both of us individually. Our incredible connection with Spirit and our own personal growth that had taken place on this wonderful spiritual journey at The Casa. It certainly was something I was never going to forget. Michael had decided he was to stay on at The Casa for a little while yet. I wished him well and said "Goodbye." I returned to my villa at 8.30pm.

During the evening I connected to Spirit expecting to connect to either the Psychic Surgeons or to my main spirit guide but to my amazement The Casa Entity Dom Inácio gently came to me, I thanked him for coming forward and I said to him,
"I was pleased to have connected to John of God today". "Yes."
"Was there anything else we needed to do to help him?" "Yes."
"Do you wish for us to send him distant healing?" "Yes."
So that's what we needed to do! The Casa Entities were going to use 'me' as their channel so that 'they' could send healing to their Medium, John of God. Well how incredible was that?
I didn't know it could be done like that but it now all made sense.
All the occasions the Entities had come to me, they were practicing and getting me used to their energies for this moment.

I got into bed at 10pm and chose a photograph of John of God that I had taken of him earlier that day.

We would be using this photograph to send the distant healing to him. I connected to the Psychic Surgeons and once they were in my hands I asked,

"Is it appropriate now for the Casa Entities to come forward to Paula?" *"Yes."*

I asked the Psychic Surgeons if they could please connect me with them and so I waited and within a few seconds I felt their gentle arrival as I connected again first of all with The Casa Entity Dom Inácio, I asked,

"Had John of God's higher self, given permission for us to proceed?" "Yes."

My hands were placed over the photograph of John of God and then The Entity began the healing.

Just as the Psychic Surgeons do, to move my hands for their healing, the Casa Entities were doing the same, without my effort they were moving my hands back and forth over the photograph of John of God. There were many blockages to be released and to clear away. With my hands we just kept pulling and pulling and pulling, out negative blockages.

There was so much being removed that the Entities were using me to 'yawn out' the blocked energy to be removed.

I channeled the white Universal light and my hands were being moved faster and faster over his photograph. Then my fingers started twirling round and round getting faster and faster as we energised John of God. The Entities then placed two of my fingers down the central chakra line of his body, they worked and worked my hands faster and faster, their energy in my own hands was immense. There was so much releasing being done by the Entities. Finally, after what had seemed like ages the Entities had finished. They had taken fifty minutes to cleanse and clear and give John of God healing.

I asked Dom Inácio, "Have we finished now?" "Yes."
"Will the healing help him?" "Yes."
"Is this a one-off healing?" "No."
"Do you wish me to send him distant healing on a regular basis?" "Yes."
"Would this be with the Psychic Surgeons?" "Yes."
"How many Casa Entities were working through me on John of God this evening please?" "4"
"When I am back in the UK will The Casa Entities come and work through me there?" "No."
"So, this evening is the last time we will work together?" "No."
"I look forward to the next time we work together whenever that may be, thank you." "Yes."

After the Casa Entities had left my body I called upon the Psychic Surgeons to come forward into my hands. I asked them if all had gone well, and they were very pleased embracing my face as if with thanks. The Psychic Surgeons then proceeded to cleanse and clear me after this amazing distant healing session.

As I lay in my bed, I put my hands together into the prayer position and I thanked all The Casa Entities for coming forward this evening, and for the healing that they had given to me whilst at The Casa. I thanked the Divine Angels that I had been working with during my time here in Brazil, and for their beautiful message. I thanked the Psychic Surgeons for guiding me to make this most amazing spiritual journey and for all their healing and guidance that I had received. I felt very emotional as I thanked them all and a few tears rolled down my cheeks with gratitude.

My return journey home was without incident. I slept for most of the flight from Brazil to Portugal and then refreshed, took the connecting flight to Heathrow airport.

Landing back in the UK where most of the snow had gone and the roads to take me home were now clear.

I continued with the Psychic Surgeons to send distant healing to John of God for many weeks after my return to the UK just as I had been asked to do and when asking the Psychic Surgeons "Was John of God receiving our healing?" *"Yes"* was their reply.

I count myself so very lucky to be on such an incredible spiritual path, to be guided in this way, and to be looked after by the Psychic Surgeons. This visit to Brazil really did take me out of my comfort zone, travelling so far on my own, yet meeting people on the way to help me. I put my trust in them and they never let me down.

This has not been the only spiritual journey I've needed to make, there are and will be more to come. It would seem that the different journeys, whether they are for my own rest and relaxation or guided journeys, all have a spiritual connection for me. I am truly blessed.

I would like to share with you my next spiritual journey, this time to Mexico.

Mexico 2019

Thinking that I would be returning to Brazil sooner rather than later, I decided to keep free in my diary two weeks in February 2019 to allow for such a trip to take place. But when asking the Psychic Surgeons for guidance they informed me I would not be going to Brazil in this year. So, I thought to myself well in that case I will have a two-week holiday instead, just for me. I looked to see where would be nice and warm and sunny and with places of interest to visit too. Mexico caught my eye and of course the Mayan's history was something I wanted to learn more about and so I booked my holiday. I thought that I would book some excursions of interest whilst I was away and decided to book a guided tour to the famous pyramid that is the Temple of Kukulkan at Chichén Itzá, which is in the Yucatan peninsula of Mexico. As my hotel was in Cancun, it was approximately a three-hour drive on the coach. My main spirit guide had indicated to me that there was something spiritual for me at Chichén Itzá, so I was very excited to be going.

I had only been in Mexico for a few days when this excursion day arrived. An early morning start, as the tour guide wanted for us to arrive before the heat of the day. On our arrival we disembarked from the coach and the tour guide took us on a walk through the jungle paths, yes, jungle paths! There had even been a road sign on our way in the coach which said, 'Beware Jaguars' and they were not referring to the car! We arrived safely at the site, which was a ruined ancient city, it was much larger than I was aware of, as it covered an area of 4 square miles.

There were many more points of interest on the site too, an observatory, a wall for the day of the dead, intricate stone carvings and a sports ball court. We were told it would take approximately three hours to tour the complex. I discovered that this ancient city was the centre of 'pilgrimage' for the ancient Maya for over one thousand years. I wondered if this was why I needed to be visiting this place.

On our arrival our guide José, led us straight to the main pyramid, the Temple of Kukulkan. He gave the group some very interesting historical facts and then we were informed he would leave us for approximately fifteen minutes to have a walk around, take photographs, and then we would meet up to move further around the complex.

(Temple of Kukulkan at Chichén Itzá and Paula at Chichén Itzá)

This was my chance, I had time on my own (not that I was 'on my own' as there were quite a few people nearby). Standing in front of the pyramid I asked the Psychic Surgeons to come forward into my hands and I asked them,

"Where I am standing, is this where I should be?" *"Yes."*
"Am I to receive an upgrade whilst I am here at Chichén Itzá?" *"Yes."*
With their confirmation the Psychic Surgeons started moving my hands, they placed them onto the top of my head onto my crown chakra, I could feel tingles as they did so. This continued for a couple of minutes, then the Psychic Surgeons moved my hands down to my heart chakra and there was a great pressure on my chest whilst this was happening. I carried on as if I was alone at the site, no one came to bother me, it really did feel very private.
When the Psychic Surgeons had finished, I asked them,
"Had I lived a previous life here?" *"Yes."*
"Were you healing a past life for me today?" *"Yes."*
"Is everything rebalanced for me now?" *"Yes."*

I thanked the Psychic Surgeons and as soon as they had left my hands, I turned around to look for my tour guide José. He was standing underneath the shade of a tree with several people from our group. As I approached them, I wondered if anyone would say anything to me, but no one did, which was great. We continued around the site, José was extremely knowledgeable and had a good sense of humour too. It made the day so enjoyable. True to his word the tour finished three hours after it had begun, by this time the sun was hot in the sky at midday and there were many more visitors arriving making the complex very busy.

The group returned to the coach and we were driven to a remote restaurant that was near to a clear blue underground cenote (sink hole). We were invited to take a swim, but I declined. Some of the group did get changed into their swimwear and took a plunge, into what was freezing cold water. I was very glad I decided not to go in after all. We then had a delicious Mexican style lunch and returned to the coach ready for our three-hour drive back to the hotel.

Once back in my hotel room I showered and changed for dinner. Did I feel any different from my upgrade experience today? No, I still felt the same, but I know that a past life clearing had been completed which would allow my healing to be more refined than ever before when I returned to the UK.

Coba Maya

The next excursion I had booked myself onto was to visit the Coba Maya pyramid. Another pyramid, there seemed a connection as to why I would be visiting two pyramids on this trip. Again being part of the Mayan culture I wondered if there would be a spiritual connection to this place, so, I asked my main spirit guide if this was the case, "Was there anything special for me there?" "No."
Oh well, never mind I'm going anyway and was looking forward to the trip.

Again, it was an early start for me, because people travelling in the group that day had to be collected from different hotels by the coach before we even started our main journey. It was actually a nice way to see the other hotels and their grounds that were in the local vicinity to my own hotel.

In the Yucatán peninsula, the city of Coba was an ancient city that had been abandoned in the 1500s. The pyramid we had come to see was called Ixmoja and was amongst one of the tallest pyramids in the region at 148 feet high.

In addition to this, it was a stepped pyramid which the general public were permitted to climb. Definitely no health and safety precautions here! Our tour guide walked us through the jungle paths, pointing out elevated ant's nests high up in the trees above us.

Our guide allowed us time to take photographs of the fauna and flora on the way before finally arriving at the pyramid site.

Initially, not as spectacular to look at as Chichén Itzá but the novelty factor of being able to climb the pyramid steps got people excited. I had made friends on the coach with a couple that I had seen on my previous excursion. So we stayed together for the trip and they kindly helped me by taking some photographs whilst I stood on the steps of the pyramid. (As shown.)

At first, I thought I would have a go and climb to the top of the pyramid; there were 120 steps. But, what I noticed was how high each step was, at least 12 inches in height. I really had to stretch each leg to climb up one step after the other. The second thought that crossed my mind was, well how do I get down?

I noticed running down the centre of the pyramid steps was a 'slack rope' which if it was meant to help people climb down it was neither use nor ornament. I could see that people were struggling to descend and were actually having to come down the pyramid steps on their bottom! Well, that made my decision, I am not going up there.

I only climbed three steps, and then called to my friends to take the photo please, you can see that's me with my arms waving up in the air. I then made my way down the three steps onto terra firma. It was a hot day and the temperature most days was 30c and I just thought the climb was not worth it. My friends and I found a log bench in the shade to sit on and watched people climbing up and down the pyramid. Once everyone from our group had returned to the meeting point, the tour guide took us back to the coach. We had a packed lunch on this trip, and he handed out ice cold water bottles and our lunch which we were delighted with.

The coach then set off and took us to a beautiful location just a couple of miles away from the pyramid where there was another cenote (sink hole) but this time instead of being underground this cenote was like a clear blue pool. We had a choice to either swim in the cenote or to join our tour guide and meet the local Mexican Shaman who would be more than happy to 'bless us'. For me, there was no choice, I wanted to go and meet the Shaman to be blessed.

There were only six of us from the group and the tour guide who chose to meet the Shaman. Short in stature the Shaman looked to be in his thirties. Dressed in white and wearing brown leather sandals.

We stood in front of him as he gave blessings to us in Mexican, then he took a pottery vase which was burning white smoke and with a feather wafted the smoke over us as he did his chanting. Not a very long ceremony but one I was glad to take part in; it was a bonus to my day, and I was very pleased.

We re-joined the main group most of whom were still swimming in the beautiful clear waters of the cenote, which was surrounded by lush greenery and palm trees; it made a beautiful setting.

Once everyone had finished and were ready to leave, our tour guide took us in the coach to a local village so we could see how the local people lived. The ladies of the village showed us how they made Tortillas on their barbeque fires, and we were then shown how to make some too. Then we were taken to the obligatory shop, where handmade goods from the village were for sale. I purchased two leather painted bookmarks as a keep sake of my day. We returned to the coach where our tour guide handed out more ice cool water bottles and afternoon cake. As I returned to my hotel, I reflected that I had had a wonderful day.

Tulum Ancient Ruins

On the second week of my stay in Mexico I had booked another two tours. The first one being a visit to the Tulum Ancient Ruins that were well known for its well-preserved ruins of an ancient Mayan port city by the sea. We were driven there by coach. We had a lady tour guide who was very knowledgeable about the ruins and made it all sound so interesting.

On our arrival we had to walk quite a way from the coach park until we reached the walled city. As we walked, on each side of the road was very thick lush green vegetation. We had to enter the 13th century walled city through a narrow doorway into beautifully kept and preserved grounds. There were many low level buildings, and a Tower or clifftop Castillo.

115

We were guided to follow the coastal path which afforded us beautiful views of the Caribbean Sea and beautiful sandy beaches below us. The tour guide took us to points of interest around the site and then gave us free time of an hour to visit ruins of our own choice. The day was hot; but the sea breeze was very welcome.

The city of Tulum served as a port for Coba, and I thought it coincidental that I should have been at the Coba Maya pyramid only a few days before. It was a lovely excursion to take, not a spiritual one but so interesting to hear about the Mayans. On our return to the coach the tour guide asked us to meet her outside the massive souvenir shop and if you arrived back early enough, you would have time to shop if you so desired. And of course, I desired. (She laughs).

The Dolphins and Healing

I was very excited about my second and last tour that week as I was about to swim with the Dolphins, something that I had always wanted to do. The tour I had booked was to exceed all my expectations of swimming with these wonderful intelligent creatures. An early start again, as on previous tours but this time in a much smaller minibus. There were only two other hotel pick-ups to make and then we were on our way to Xel-Há, which was the name of an eco-friendly all-inclusive water park.

116

Where everything is set up to reduce your footprint as a visitor and make the least amount of impact on the environment and its inhabitants; I loved this idea.

Our tour guide for the day took us through the park entrance and towards the Delphinus area where the Dolphins were. On our arrival to this area we were asked to change into our swimwear ready to swim with the Dolphins at 9.30am. We were to remove all jewellery and put on a life jacket, which was to help with additional buoyancy in the water. We were paired up with other people to make groups of four wherever possible. I was teamed up with a father and son who were from Manchester. We were led to an enclosed pool and down some ladder steps to a wooden submerged platform, where we waited for the experience to begin.

Already in the water was the Dolphin's trainer equipped with his whistle and a box of fish treats for the Dolphin. Then suddenly the Dolphin appeared in the water right in front of us. It was a male Dolphin; he was massive and must have been 8 feet long or more!
I was just inches away from this beautiful creature, I hoped I would be allowed to touch him. We were asked to swim into the centre of the pool where the Dolphin swam around us at high speed, then splashing us on purpose with his tail, and then jumping over us several times. We then swam back to the wooden platform where the Dolphin then swam in front of us and the trainer encouraged us to touch him, but not to touch the Dolphin near the blowhole or his dorsal fin. His skin felt like a wet chamois leather very silky and soft. The Dolphin then proceeded to swim back and forth in front of us, first on his back allowing us to stroke his tummy, then splashing us with his tail. Then, each of us in turn were given solo time with the Dolphin. When it was my turn, I had to swim out into the pool again and the Dolphin swam around me, allowing me to stroke him as he passed.

I wondered if, with the help of the Psychic Surgeons we were giving the Dolphin healing, it transpired that the Dolphin was actually giving healing to me! How beautiful was that? There was an official photographer at the side of the pool.

I was asked to gently hold the Dolphin and then the trainer instructed the Dolphin to come in closer, they said "You may kiss the Dolphin if you wish," which of course I had no hesitation in doing. His nose felt like wet velvet on my lips. After that wonderful moment, we were all asked to swim out into the centre of the pool again and line up in a row. Suddenly, the Dolphin jumped right out of the water over our heads and into the water in front of us. It wasn't until he did this jump that I could see just how large the Dolphin was. That jump was the finale to our swim with the Dolphin, we were asked to swim back to the wooden platform, where we exited the pool. We made our way to the changing rooms, and when everyone was ready, we were all gathered together as a group and asked to return to the pool area for 1.30pm ready for the next experience with the Dolphins. How exciting, I couldn't wait.

With a good couple of hours to myself I made my way to the all-inclusive restaurant as all that swimming had given me an appetite. The choice of food was incredible; and the food on display was all the colours of the rainbow. It also made sense to eat now, so that my lunch was digested in plenty of time before my next Dolphin experience.

After I left the restaurant, I followed the signs to see The Manatee, referred to as the water mermaid. I wanted to be able to get up close and see what these creatures were like. A long and winding walk through beautifully planted areas, I arrived at the Manatee pools and looked down from the observation areas to see if I could see one. In the water all I could see was what looked like giant grey boulders at the bottom of a sandy pool. Then gently one of the boulders moved very slowly through the water. I laughed; I had actually been looking at a Manatee all the time, but it had been motionless at the bottom of the pool. To describe them as looking like a boulder is a perfect description with lumps and bumps growing on their green-grey coloured backs.

I noticed that the animal trainers were starting to put out the Manatees lunch throwing green leaves and vegetables into the water, suddenly there was more movement! The Manatee knew it was feeding time and they ever so slowly moved through the water, their enormous fan like tail moving them towards their food. I was also just in time to watch a group of visitors being taken down to the water's edge to stand in line to feed the Manatee. As far as I could see there were only two Manatee in the pool, so it took ages for everyone to take a turn to feed them. I checked my watch, and it was time to make my way back to the Dolphin pools ready for my next Dolphin experience.

The next Dolphin experience I was about to take part in, was something that was almost unbelievable for me, (I'm not really a very sporty person) but I was going to be diving with the Dolphins. Yes, diving! I was going to take part in a 'Sea TREK®' glass helmet underwater experience. I had always loved the idea of being underwater and viewing the marine life, seeing the colourful fishes, but scuba diving made me nervous, with the air tanks etc.

So this was my opportunity to still take part. There was no previous experience required, which was great.

The Sea TREK experience entailed a glass domed divers' helmet being placed over my head and resting on my shoulders. The dome allowed me a 180-degree view, there was an air tube which fed the oxygen into the glass helmet, making it so easy to breathe and best of all my face was nice and dry.

Before the group could begin this experience we had to sit and listen to a safety briefing, which gave information on the helmet and its use, descent down into the water, then we were all shown the underwater safety hand signals, and that we must follow the underwater trainers instructions at all times. We were split up into smaller groups and I joined the father and son whom I had been teamed up with previously. We followed the trainer to the water's edge, where all the glass helmets were lined up on the floor with the long air tubes attached. The trainer fitted each of us with our glass helmet and indicated that we would descend into the water one at a time. The father went first, then the son and then me.

I was instructed to descend the ladder facing inwards towards the wall of the pool and using my hands to descend on the ladder rungs, it felt wonderful, I was weightless, and I felt just like an astronaut floating around but in water! Once I reached the bottom of the ladder, I realised I was now walking on sand on the seabed. Unbelievable! I could feel the sand between my toes.

As I looked up, I could see the sun light filtering through the water. I turned around to see the others in the group were lined up holding onto the underwater handrail. The trainer was in front of us in the water and we signalled we were OK and thumbs up, ready to go.

Immediately, to my delight the Dolphin appeared, he swam in front of us at speed, around the trainer, then back and forth in front of each of us, I was looking the Dolphin in the eye underwater. It was incredible!

The trainer fed the Dolphin small fish treats which brought in towards us lots of beautiful little multicoloured fish for us to see, as these fish fed off the tiny scraps missed by the Dolphin.

With hand signals the trainer instructed us to fold our arms across our chest because the next moment the Dolphin swam passed us at speed corkscrewing his body as he swam by. The trainer rewarded him again with fish treats and the pretty little coloured fish swam up close to us again, what a joy. We were then allowed to touch the Dolphin as he slowly swam passed us.

(There was no under-water photography, so I have used this advertising image crediting Sea-Trek.com to show the glass helmets that were used).

Photograph credits Sea-Trek.com

Then each of us were given the opportunity to interact with the Dolphin individually. Using only my two fingers and waving them in the water, as if I was a Conductor, the Dolphin responded to me by singing in the water with bubbles coming out of his blowhole. Finally, the trainer instructed the Dolphin to stand upright with his tail on the seabed. Only at this point do you realise just how long the Dolphin is when he is 'standing' alongside you.

It was now time to exit the water and as I walked along the seabed to the ladder, I felt quite emotional by all that I had seen. I floated up to the surface, where an assistant was waiting to remove my helmet for me. I waited for the others to emerge and we just couldn't stop talking we were so excited! We were all blown away by this amazing experience. I was so happy with all that had taken place that day, but the trainer said to us, "Come this way there is more," "More?" I thought that was it!

The trainer beckoned us to follow him along the wooden boardwalks towards another pool. I call them pools, but really these were like giant salt water lakes that the Dolphins swam in.
The rest of our original group were gathered waiting for us, I wondered what was happening. Then we were handed a snorkel and mask, we were going to snorkel with the mother and baby Dolphins. OMG! I am beyond excited.

We all got into the water and then the Dolphins arrived, I think there were four mothers and four babies swimming around us. We were allowed to touch them if they swam near to us, but the babies were quite skittish and avoided any touch preferring to swim next to their mum. Using my mask, I put my face into the water and to my delight I could hear the Dolphins communicating with each other hearing their clicks in the water. How magical was this? My day just couldn't get any better, but I have to say it did!

We got out of the water and handed back our masks. We were then directed to walk further along the boardwalk to another pool and waited...

Our final encounter with the Dolphins was to be the most spectacular! We were instructed that two Dolphins were going to join us in this pool. We would be taking it in turns, and I was to go first. I was instructed that once in the water, I was to lock my knees and keep my legs completely straight and then hold my arms out to the side.
The two Dolphins would then swim up underneath me and each Dolphin would touch one foot and push me up and through the water. OMG! Don't they know how old I am to be doing this? (She laughs).

I didn't have time to think about it, before I knew it, I felt the Dolphins nose on my feet, and whoosh I was being pushed up out of the water and being pushed along the pool. With water splashing in my face everything was a blur, I could just about see one of the trainers at the side of the pool shouting, "Hold your arms out," ha ha, easier said than done I thought. I was being pushed along at quite a speed it really was quite exhilarating and I was so enjoying it so much and smiling from ear to ear. Then I could feel we were slowing down in the water and the Dolphins moved away from my feet back to their trainer. I was left in the centre of the pool to swim to the exit ladder. Not an easy task when you are wearing a life jacket. The others in the group did much better than I had, especially the men, but I did feel sorry for the lady who was wearing a bikini, it didn't stay up for very long!

I wasn't aware that the official photographer was poolside taking photographs but to my delight he had captured my wonderful experience, as you can see below.

We had been told that these were second generation captive Dolphins that we were interacting with that day. I wondered if being in captivity like this was detrimental to their wellbeing, knowing what intelligent mammals they were, so, I asked the Psychic Surgeons,
"Are these Dolphins being well looked after?" "Yes."
"Were these Dolphins sad?" "No."
"Are these Dolphins helping people?" "Yes."
"Are these Dolphins healing people who come to visit?" "Yes."
There was nothing more to say, these beautiful creatures were helping the many, many people who came to see them, to interact with them, to touch them, to swim with them and I was privileged to be one of them that day and it was magical.

(The lovely Dolphin posing and then jumping over me.)

~ ~ ~ ~ ~

St Michael's Cave, Gibraltar

The Easter of 2019 I booked myself on a long weekend to Gibraltar. It was time for me to have a rest from the healing and recharge my own batteries. I had only been to Gibraltar briefly once before on a day trip from Spain. This time I wanted to see the sights, take a ride on the cable car, visit the top of the Rock and see the monkeys. More interestingly though, I wanted to visit the spectacular St Michael's Cave. I had heard so much about it and how beautiful it was, and my main spirit guide had indicated to me that there was something special for me there. Should I choose to visit I would be receiving a spiritual upgrade. Try keeping me away!

After arriving at my hotel I asked in Reception about getting to and from the Rock from the hotel, which was by the local bus service. So after I unpacked I checked the timetable and waited outside the hotel and took the local bus to the cable car station.

This was where you paid for your cable car ride but also your entrance ticket for the Upper Rock Nature Reserve, where St Michael's Cave was situated. A lovely ride to the top of the Rock and a great opportunity to take scenic photographs. The cave was situated 300 metres above sea level and in ancient times the cave was known to the Greeks and the Romans. Getting out of the cable car I noticed a restaurant where I took the opportunity to sit and have a cup of tea and plan my day.

First of all, I had to manoeuvre myself passed the Apes who were known to pounce on visitors especially those with bags or carrier bags. The Apes now associated these with containing food for them. It is against regulations to feed them. I held onto my handbag tightly. As luck would have it the Apes had just been fed, with many of them eating on fresh fruit, oranges, bananas and pieces of apple. With their preoccupation I was able to get passed them with ease and even managed to take a couple of photos for the album.

I continued on the path sign posted to St Michael's Cave, it was only 800 yards walk from the cable car, but it was mainly down a steep hill but with wonderful scenery views on the way.

I arrived at the cave kiosk and with only a short queue now found myself inside the cave entrance. Down a short flight of steps, to what I can only describe as a 'wow' moment. There in front of me, was the cavernous Cathedral Cave. I had heard that it was magnificent to see with coloured spotlights lighting up the enormous stalactites and stalagmites. It didn't disappoint.

There were rows and rows of seating, as this place was used as an auditorium because of the wonderful acoustics. It seated approximately 400 people. As I stood there marvelling at the kaleidoscope of ever-changing colours on these colossal columns; I could see why it was known as one of the most spectacular natural grottos in Europe. There was no specific route to follow but footpaths took you in the directions of columns and formations of interest. Some clearly had faces within them, others had animal images, there was even one of Queen Victoria with a crown on her head. The lighting was out of this world.

The spotlight colours going from red to pink to orange to yellow to green and blue and then violet. As the colours changed so too did the images within the columns.

I found a pathway leading up to a flight of steps and a viewing platform which rewarded me with another cavern full of stalactites and stalagmites. Only this time illuminated with a pale cream spotlight that created enormous shadows that reflected images across to the opposite cave walls.

As there was no one around I connected to the Psychic Surgeons and asked them,

"Is this area where I need to be to receive my spiritual upgrade?"

"No."

"Is the special place I need to stand in further on into the caves?"

"Yes."

I continued following the various footpaths leading me to points of interest, some that took me down flights of steps as well as up. I took loads of photographs along the way capturing these incredible images. But I could see I was getting near to the end of the footpaths towards the exit.

So, I stopped again, and I asked the Psychic Surgeons,

"Have I reached the place that I need to be yet?" *"No."*

"Is the special place nearby?" *"Yes."*

Sure enough, just around the corner of a large protruding boulder, was a small dimly lit glass fronted balcony. I peered over the edge, oh my goodness me, it was a black bottomless pit going deep down into Mother Earth. I stood back, could this be the place? I needed to ask the Psychic Surgeons for their guidance.

"Is this the special place I need to be?" *"Yes."*

Fantastic, as the Psychic Surgeons were already in my hands, I asked them to proceed. They placed my hands on the top of my head, just as they had done in Mexico at Chichén Itzá and proceeded to give me my latest spiritual upgrade. A few minutes went by and then they were finished. I thanked them for this wonderful gift, that could only be given to me in this place in this precise spot.

I was later to find out that the Elementals had joined in with the Psychic Surgeons for this ceremony and this made perfect sense to me, as I had been in the bowels of the Earth in these wonderful caves, where else could be better?

I made my way back to the Cathedral cave and took a seat in the second row of the seating. As I sat and drank my water, I wanted to savour this magical place just one more time before departing. My eyes scanned the columns again, it was as if I could see faces looking at me! Some happy and smiling some not so happy. In the distance I could see a face that looked like that of a deer. I got my camera out and took several photos of it to hopefully capture the face that I could see. It was now time to leave, I had been in the caves for more than two hours.

I made my way to the exit and out into the fresh air. I stopped for a cold drink before having to face the steep climb back up the hill to the cable car station. I took my time, I was in no rush, and took photographs of the views. Down below where I was standing, I could see the port of Gibraltar where two cruise liner ships were docked, and there were big container ships on the horizon waiting to come into port. In addition to these there were many pleasure boats too, that needed a photograph taking of them. As I made my way up the hill, I started to notice some of the Apes were ahead of me, some were sunning themselves on the footpath, others were sitting in groups. I kept my head down as I passed them not wishing to be a target of their attention.

It was a hot day, the sky was clear and blue, and I was needing some more refreshment. I arrived at the cable car station and restaurant and in front of me I could see the most fantastic views of Gibraltar, Spain, the Mediterranean Sea, the Straits of Gibraltar and in the distance, views of Morocco and Africa.

I made a beeline for the restaurant and had a long refreshing drink and a light lunch. I took some more photographs because these were going to be a fantastic keepsake of my trip here.

I made my way back to the cable car and was soon descending down the Rock face to the lower levels, where the Botanical Gardens called La Alameda were situated. Entry into these beautiful gardens was free and what a delight they were. So many unusual plants and trees, like the Dragon tree, and many flowers that were in bloom much earlier than the UK, which attracted different species of birds and butterflies. The gardens were built to promote the continued development and conservation as well as education and enjoyment for the people of Gibraltar.

After I had finished walking around the gardens, I took a bus ride back to my hotel, and as I reflected on all that had happened it had been another magical day and another magical trip.

I find it incredible that now, wherever I go, I am actually going on a spiritual journey of some kind. The Psychic Surgeons have many plans for me in the future and I can't wait!

7. Sir Arthur Conan Doyle

Quote
"There is no scent so pleasant to my nostrils as that faint,
subtle reek which comes from an ancient book."
~ Sir Arthur Conan Doyle ~

It was such a great honour....

Today is an extremely exciting day for me! It is the day when at last I am to be connected to Sir Arthur Conan Doyle for him to channel his messages through me. The Psychic Surgeons had guided me that the month of November would be the right time for the connection to be made. I linked to the Psychic Surgeons and as they stepped forward from their dimension and through into my hands, I was greeted as always with an embrace to my face. I asked them, "Psychic Surgeons, was today the day for this special connection?" *"Yes"* they replied. I was so excited as it had been over a year since I had been informed that Sir Arthur was going to write through me. I had saved a notepad and pen especially for this momentous event and I was ready.

I asked the Psychic Surgeons if they would please bring Sir Arthur Conan Doyle forward through into my hands as we had arranged. I waited a few seconds and then my hands began to move, I then said out loud, "Good morning is that Sir Arthur Conan Doyle in my hands?" My face was again embraced but this time with his greeting. I picked up my pen in my left hand and it began to move with the automatic writing forming the following words.

"I am here my dear I am Sir Arthur, greetings to you dear Paula I have waited for a long time to help you. It is a good day. For us to begin I want you to write with your right hand." (Previously he had asked to write with my natural left hand.) "That is better, I can move the pen easier. I am going to begin..." And so the connection I had waited so long for was now beginning, he continued...

"I am Sir Arthur Conan Doyle I have come forward to channel through our dear Paula. To begin, I am of the opinion that this world has forgotten Spirit. Yes, there are those of you who are spiritual, and this is not directed at you."

"In my lifetime in the early twentieth century people attended church every Sunday. But modern day life has taken over and you have lost your way and without Spirit in your lives you are lost. We need to help and guide you, but you do not listen. We find it so difficult to connect with the Human Race to help and guide you all. There are times when, by listening, you would have been saved from much turmoil and sadness. But we in Spirit understand this and we wait until you are ready to receive our guidance. I am here to add to our dear Paula's book with words of guidance for you all. You already know my reputation as a writer, and I have attended many circles in the past to give guidance. I've been in Spirit for the last ninety years and I have learnt much from this side of life and it is my intention to share some of this knowledge with you."

"I wish to impart the following guidance to you. See with your own eyes what is going on in the world. Do not be dictated to by others, go within, you already know the answers. You are seeing many changes and there are more to come. Unfortunately, the Human Race has taken the long road, as without spiritual guidance you have had to find your own way and we know it has not been easy."

"We observe you from above and watch you plunder the planet of her resources never replenishing enough for what has been taken. We watch as some of you try to help the animal kingdom and watch as different species become extinct. This is not how it was meant to be. You were meant to flourish and preserve, now the planet is in decline, it is so sad to observe. We in Spirit can guide you, if only you would listen."

"The pandemic of 2020 served as a wakeup call to you all. It was seen that through a reduction in manufacturing the planet started to heal. But you are returning to your 'old ways' and the planet, she suffers again. This was your wake up call, some of you listened and some did not. It will be the dark before the dawn. We in Spirit have many channels like our dear Paula whom we can use to bring forth our guidance and to this end, I Sir Arthur offer you guidance. It is many years since I last wrote a book and this process of writing through Paula is a delight even if it is a challenge. The nature of my guidance is tenfold and there are many subjects for me to cover, I am writing to share the knowledge I have attained in my time here in Spirit, so it is with my love that I begin to channel the following to you."

"We want you to know that the planet cannot sustain all of the people without there being a detrimental effect on the planet Earth. We need to inform you of the possible changes that could happen, for the betterment of the planet and those that live upon it. We will be here to help and guide you through these dark days and many of you will turn to Spirit, for guidance to ask for help. The help is there it always has been."

"There are many people 'awakening' to see what is happening and through this they will begin to work together. Everything comes from love. We all come with love in our hearts to you all. We need more love. Love is the only vibration on which to build, not war. We in Spirit are unconditional love, we are one. So many of you are separated and alone. We need you to be together as one as Spirit intended. Only through a decrease in numbers will this then bring people together, love will bond you all together."

"With guidance from Spirit you can achieve this, we can help you, through your change in attitude and your change in caring for the planet. Listen to those who already speak out. Their words are our words, they speak the truth of what is happening, they are our voice. It is most important that you listen, time is running out, there is much that can be done now, you must listen. I need you to take notice of my message it is so important. You all have a choice, currently, the Human Race is choosing the easy way, but because of this, the future will be very hard for you all. Through my words I need you to take action. Change your ways, the resources you take for granted now are running out. Change how you heat your home, change your transportation. Change how you treat your part in this world, the food you eat, grow your own, put your own home grown food on the table. Be part of the sustainable future. We know you can do it. Flowers are lovely but grow more produce for you and your family to eat. Rely less on mass farming of foods and add your own produce to help financially and economically too."

"We have seen the pride many of you had at sharing the produce you had grown in the year of 2020. When too much of a certain food had been harvested, you began sharing with those who were less fortunate, this is what we all need to do."

"We in Spirit welcome this change it pulls everyone together as a community and no longer as individuals, but together as a group pulling and working together looking after each other in times of need."

"This has to be highlighted to you all, materialism will diminish, possessions will no longer be the priority. Only food, warmth, and a roof over your head are the priorities. Bartering from the days of old will return when we exchange that which no longer serves us for food and tools, to then provide you with your own crops. My words will not fall on deaf ears, some people are starting to sit up and listen already and this pleases me."

"We in Spirit wish it to be known that through it all we are still here to help and guide you. Meditation is the best way to connect to us and we will guide you through thought and through visual signs. Each person interprets the messages differently, no one is wrong. Each of you are on your own path no one else should compare to you, each one of you lives their path and no one else's. Jealousy is a very negative vibration but one that if 'rife' in the spiritual community, it is not what we would wish. Do not envy others for their success. Spirit has chosen each of you to follow your own path not that of another. Together each individual has the ability to help another. Do not let jealousy get the better of you, when in doubt seek guidance from your guides or Angels. Ask for them to help you to see the best in everyone. We are all working towards one goal, that we become one in unity, working together, we each have a contribution to make. Make yours count, however small. This is your role, your path, be guided for the best outcome for all."

"Our dear Paula has had to deal with those who are jealous of her connection to the Psychic Surgeons. Paula has a greater responsibility to help beyond the planet, beyond the Human Race. She has been chosen for the work she needs to do. Do not envy her, do not delay her, help her for she is chosen."

135

"Many people are amazed at the world of Spirit and that is also true for our dear Paula, even though all of these experiences are happening to her, she remains humbled by her destiny and her connection to Spirit."

"What I am trying to say is, respect those that have an important role to play, we need people like Paula to help our cause to make this world a better and healthier place to be. So do all you can, help each other."

"In these times of uncertainty the family is the most important thing, but due to distance and living apart, you are often unable to see your loved ones. Please include each and every one in your prayers at night. Spirit are listening, you need to have faith and trust that all will be well. My dear ones it is from my experience from both sides of life that I can share this with you."

"With my knowledge I wish to impart the following, I Sir Arthur, wrote many novels and spiritual scriptures during my life, but nothing prepared me for the beauty of what was ahead of me in Spirit. I am going to share with you some of the miracles of healing that takes place continually night and day. With many healing energies in Spirit, healing is being carried out all over the Universe not just here on your Earth. There are many Psychic Surgeons in Spirit working through channels such as our dear Paula, giving healing on a daily basis. As a Physician myself, I watch the Psychic Surgeons and Doctors gifted in this magnificent way, I am in wonder at their skill and level of care, in awe of what they do to help all. The Psychic Surgeons are from many different era's and each bring to the operating table a wealth of knowledge and experience in different medical areas. Even in Spirit the Psychic Surgeons are learning, being taught by those even more knowledgeable than they, so that the healing can be applied to those in need, especially at a distance."

"There has and always will be miraculous healings taking place where healing cannot be explained scientifically, but that continue to take place up to present day. I watch the Psychic Surgeons and Doctors gain more knowledge in their healing techniques and how they teach and instruct their channel our dear Paula in helping the patients in their return to wellness."

"The Psychic Surgeons are of a generation where medicine was in its infancy but in Spirit they now exceed today's medical practitioners in knowledge and capability without the need for external surgery to take place. The Psychic Surgeons work on a different vibration to those on this planet therefore achieving results way beyond the knowledge of today. The Psychic Surgeons are assisted by helpers and other multidimensional beings in the healing and what they can achieve is truly wonderous. I am so pleased to see that this type of spiritual surgery healing is being more widely accepted by the general public worldwide."

"We in Spirit are extremely pleased with all that is being achieved and with channels like our dear Paula, she is helping to increase people's awareness of this healing modality, as so much of the healing can be done without having to attend the hospitals. There are now many modern day Doctors and Surgeons joining the Psychic Surgeons Team, bringing with them new modern ways of working that educates the other Psychic Surgeons to a better way to operate on the patient. So much is achieved in a healing session, whether in person through their channel or by distant healing through their channel."

"I was before, a man of many abilities, I was a Physician as well as an Author. I am pleased that I can share with you more insights but also share with you the healing that is now taking place through the channel Paula. She is a beautiful person with only good intentions for people's wellbeing. She is committed to helping so many people on her own healing journey."

"In Spirit, the Psychic Surgeons love her dearly for the work she does. In return the Psychic Surgeons are applying healing through her, greater than there has ever been seen before. She works at a very high vibration and this enables the Psychic Surgeons to carry out Psychic Surgery way beyond that of other channels. She is pure of heart and, has a kind heart. People are drawn to her as she has a kindness that is not very often seen."

"She has a softly spoken healing voice, because of this, those in Spirit are also drawn to her. I have watched our dear Paula since my connection with her last year and have nothing but admiration for her work and her dedication. But enough 'patting on her back' for now."

"I Sir Arthur, come forward to share the most amazing healing story that has taken place from the beautiful hands of our dear Paula. There was an occasion when the healing was needed from the Psychic Surgeons, when a lady came to Paula to ask for healing. Without Paula's knowledge this lady was dying, but the Psychic Surgeons had guided her to Paula as they knew they could help her. The healing was given to the lady who had a serious life threatening condition, and the Psychic Surgeons were able to give her healing to save her life by releasing the mental, emotional and physical blockages so that the lady's body was able to start healing itself back to wellness. To this day, Paula is unaware of 'who' this lady may have been and of the incredible healing that took place, but I wanted it to be known for this book."

"I have acquired much knowledge in Spirit and have this to share with you dear readers. In my last incarnation as Sir Arthur Conan Doyle I wrote many spiritual scriptures, and I am of the opinion that people need to be more open to what is transpiring, and I can help to open your eyes to this new way of thinking. The idea that we do not exist after the physical body 'dies' is false. Our spirit leaves the physical body to return to Spirit to where we truly belong."

"Myself, I am very happy here in Spirit. To be one is all that we are. To ascend further there are certain tasks we have to carry out to help new spirits into the realms of being and help with their adjustment, just as I was adjusted on my arrival into Spirit in 1930. I have ascended many times and will continue to do so."

"Many of you who read this book will already be 'open' and willing to learn but these messages need to be passed on to others for them to open up to Spirit and I hope you will do this for our dear Paula for she has devoted her later life in helping others, whether through the Psychic Surgeons healing or through the inspirational words in her books."

"From the turn of the new century 2000 you have experienced many changes whether by climate change, by political change or by your own voting for change. From these changes there is a new way of life forming and through these changes you are learning to adapt. Helping the planet Earth is a major consideration for everyone as the planet moves into the new vibration of the Age of Aquarius. We in Spirit are helping and guiding you with these changes, some people listen, and some do not. This has to be shared with you all, it is of the utmost importance that you are guided into action with the messages given. Heart love is something each of you must achieve if you are to progress. I do not say this lightly, I am a messenger myself. You all know my reputation as a spiritual writer, and I am being guided to pass these messages on to you. Followers of my previous work will know my words."

"I Sir Arthur Conan Doyle, am of the opinion that in the modern world today there is too much technology, too much mis-information that is now confusing to all. Spirit do not wish for this to continue and you will see changes in this area, there will be less not more! The technology will not disappear altogether, but things will change from how you know it today."

"There will be a going back to nature just as you experienced in the year of 2020 but first you must secure the longevity of the planet Earth and do everything you can to help her. You need this planet to survive and in return she will bless you with her beauty and her bounty. Nature will provide for you but you all need to play your part."

"You must give, do not keep taking, the planet cannot sustain this without replenishment. Many of you have already recognised this and are doing your part but you need to recruit many others to help. Many hands make light work, please bare this in mind. If you listen, if you act now, more can be achieved. The planet will respond she will provide your food, your shelter, your comfort, and your piece of mind. Act now to save your planet for it is all that you have. Abuse it and you will lose it. This guidance if acted upon will save much future hardship and much loss of life. We in Spirit do not wish to see this but it is a possibility. The future really is in your hands. For we see all that is happening, changes are taking place and we are pleased with this. But not enough is being done you must step up all your efforts to help."

"For other aspects of life there are too many livestock animals on the planet by this I refer to dairy cows, sheep, pigs and cattle reared for the consumption of meat. This has to change. To embrace the changes by becoming vegetarian or vegan, eating no meat or fish is what is needed to rebalance life. We in Spirit have seen much illness from the consumption of animal flesh and this needs to change. Many people are adapting to this new way of eating and our dear channel Paula is now a vegetarian, something which she would admit she never thought she would do. It can and must be done, eating less livestock animals, with less meat consumed equates to better health for everyone and for the planet. Livestock 'spew' over fourteen percent of all greenhouse gases into the Earth's atmosphere. Less livestock can mean cleaner air and contribute to the wellness of the planet and those that live upon it."

"With the advancement of technology I can only say that I am in awe of what has been invented since my passing in 1930. All the wonderful inventions that have helped man to develop further. Unfortunately, these innovations have moved the Human Race away from nature and it's only after these many years that it has been realised that this is to the detriment of man and the planet."

"There has been no moderation and consumerism has taken over your world and gone too far. A correction needs to be made back to nature. Much of what has been developed is of no use at all to the Human Race; but is a luxury. These have their place, but not when they take over the daily aims in life. We in Spirit need to ask you to adjust your luxury standards. Refrain from modern day luxuries so that you exist more frugally and in line with nature. If more people were to take notice then the resources of the planet would be able to continue. If people do not heed this guidance then there will be consequences which we in Spirit would not wish to see."

"I am of the opinion that greed is taking over the Human Race and before it is taken away from you, why not let it be of your own accord? I believe that one day a better place can be built for all. Using this opportunity to speak on behalf of Spirit pleases me to get this important guidance to you. Be aware that if no changes take place on your part then changes will have to be made to correct the path that the Human Race is currently on. I also believe that in time the Human Race will be able to be self-sufficient as technology decreases. Many people will struggle with this new way of life, but it must be. It has to happen; change must take place. I am of the opinion that we in Spirit can help and guide you through this transition to become a more healthier generation and replenish the resources of planet Earth."

"It is of interest to you all to make changes however small, that when added together make enormous changes that can be seen and felt. Yes, this needs to be done and soon, for the good of all. Soon you will be able to see a difference if people follow this guidance. Community, a coming together, you will be a closer community as in the days of old."

"We in Spirit would like it to be known that we are concerned, as to the suitability of the world's justification into the way that the Human Race is being directed, since the pandemic took hold in the year of 2020. We would like it to be known that there are other options available without there being just one choice. There is a further choice of options available, and we would like to share these with you. I am of the opinion that the following are choices that can be made:"

* Freedom of rights is your option
* To have a choice is your right
* Be mindful of your thoughts
* Let your voice be heard

"We in Spirit would be pleased to share with you the following guidance, choose wisely, make up your own mind, go with what your own intuition tells you, that is the best and only way to move forward. Unite as one. You are stronger as one, your voice will be heard. If you can follow our guidance you will find your rights will be honoured. We guide you in this way to help you realise that you have choices. Because of this we can guide you on the right path. We are of the opinion that this is the right guidance to impart to you at this time. That all can and will be a better outcome for you all from the guidance given. We would like it to be known that all can be retrieved if you act swiftly and as one in these challenging times, and we have guided you as best we can."

"There are still challenges ahead but if you can come together there is strength in numbers. Be guided my dear friends and you will come through this together. I am of the opinion that I have said enough for now and I am happy to have passed this message across."

Footnote from Paula Jackson

I have read and understood the channeled messages and warnings that Spirit, and Sir Arthur are putting across to us regarding the future of our planet. It especially resonated with me, when I watched on BBC1 on 31st January 2021 the programme, A Perfect Planet by Sir David Attenborough. Visible proof of what is happening to the planet Earth, the changing weather patterns, the oceans, the polar caps, the animal kingdom.

Devasting changes to our climate, impacting on many countries around the world all through the actions of us Humans. The burning of fossil fuels of coal, oils and natural gas causing more CO_2 emissions and carbon dioxide into the air and the use and disposal of plastic into the oceans.

Sir Arthur wanted to use the word 'catastrophic' in his channeled messages, but I was unsure to use this word. But after having watched this programme, he was right and I was wrong, so my apologies for this. For as the programme showed, if we do not make changes now then we as a Human Race will suffer too. Time is not on our side, if we do not change our ways now, there will be no planet for our future generations.

I am not one for speaking out in this way, but Sir Arthur has taken such care to convey the message to us from Spirit to take action now and I agree. I know I will do everything in my power to change my own footprint and if I can do more, then I will. I hope you will too.

8. Sir Arthur Conan Doyle – continues..

Quote
"It is a great thing to start life with a small number of really good books which are your very own."
~ Sir Arthur Conan Doyle ~

"I want to say I am of the opinion that it is important to read as many books as is possible for the study and adjustment of one's own education. I have included in this publication, three of my quotes in my chapters, that instil the importance of owning books and their importance in communicating knowledge of a subject.

My dear Paula has kindly selected quotes for me to choose from and she was already of the opinion which ones I might choose. It was a joy to listen to my quotes being spoken again and I thank her for researching the quotes for me. Our book is developing well, and I am pleased to be able to contribute to dear Paula's book. She is a delight to work through and I am enjoying our connection immensely."

145

"I am Sir Arthur, and I am of the opinion to relay, that it is extraordinary that as I come forward to do the automatic writing through our dear Paula, that she inspires me to write a more comprehensive message for her book as I had promised to do when we first connected over one year ago. I find that after writing again after such a long time it is testing my brain! But having got back into the flow I am enjoying our connection."

"Today, to inspire you I write to say that of all the people I could have been linked to, I am so pleased it is to our dear Paula. For she inspires many with her healing path with the Psychic Surgeons and I am so pleased to be part of this."

"In the days of my previous incarnation as Sir Arthur, I wrote many spiritual scriptures, but none have compared to the incredible spiritual path that our dear Paula is on. She inspires many people with how she has come to accept the Psychic Surgeons as part of her daily life with the incredible healing that is channeled through her. She also has the responsibility to promote to the world how this healing modality can help so many. Her dedication is an inspiration to us all, for the Psychic Surgeons push her out of any comfort zone she temporarily settles into, and they push her forward to continue to grow and learn from them."

"As I Sir Arthur observe our dear Paula, I am struck by her acceptance of what is asked of her. We in Spirit love her very much and we are very proud of all she has achieved. Even allowing myself, Sir Arthur to write through her and trusting my energy in her hands. I am of the opinion that she will go far, the Psychic Surgeons have many plans for her, and I know she will embrace these because she trusts them. Trust is very important when connecting to Spirit and after ten years of working with the Psychic Surgeons our dear Paula has built up an immense trust in the Surgeons."

"Let me say that the dedication from our dear Paula is to be admired for not everyone can or will accommodate Spirit as she has. Now that her connection to the Psychic Surgeons is second nature, the Surgeons are rewarding her for her dedication and in the future she will see this come to fruition in the form of a Healing Sanctuary. (She is smiling as she reads my written words). This is something that she has wished for and Spirit have heard her. People will come to her Healing Sanctuary for the healing from the Psychic Surgeons. As the Surgeons do not wish for her to travel as much as she has done in the past, although it was necessary at the time. I know our dear Paula will be successful. There will be many new Psychic Surgeons who will come forward to work through her to give the Psychic Surgeon healing. It will be a very exciting time for her, and Spirit are pleased to reward her in this way. To see this beautiful soul grow in this way is for me Sir Arthur, an absolute delight and I will watch over her as she progresses."

"Our dear Paula is so pleased with the connection between her and I, Sir Arthur Conan Doyle that I am only too pleased to add further to her book. I have today another message to impart. I am of the opinion that in the days of old I would despair at what was taking place in the world back then. It was a time of change and a time of great hardship for those who were poor. In today's modern world you need to help the less fortunate so that they may survive the struggles that are taking place in today's world. More can and must be done to help the less fortunate. Coming together to help one another. These are great times of change and if you will be guided we in Spirit can help all concerned. It is important to share what you have with others so that all can be equal. Not everyone has the same opportunities, and this often sets the scene for their future. If you can help each other the world would be a better place. In time you will see that by sharing with each other there will be a coming together of the masses and you will unite as one. Be kind to others, share what you have, so that you all shine."

"Spirit has asked me to bring this message to you as many people are unaware that they can help each other in this way. By guiding you now you can make these important changes. We in Spirit would wish to see this in all men and women so that everyone is equal, that all is one. I Sir Arthur, would be so pleased to see this come to pass. It can be done as I spend my days in Spirit also helping others."

"It has been a pleasure writing for our dear Paula's book. I am honoured to have contributed to it and see its success. I Sir Arthur, wish that you all stay happy and healthy."

"Finally, it has come to my notice that I am remembered more for my writings of Sherlock Holmes than for my spiritual scriptures. And so to delight the readers I am writing a new short story for you all, it is called, Sherlock Holmes and the Missing Glass Slipper."
Sir Arthur Conan Doyle.

9. Sherlock Holmes and
The Missing Glass Slipper

Quote
"Nature is the true revelation of the Deity to man.
The nearest green field is the inspired page from
which you may read all that it is needful
for you to know."
~ Sir Arthur Conan Doyle ~

My dear Sherlock had in the past many enquiries for help and one such enquiry involved a missing glass slipper. The owner of said slipper had been out dancing the night before and in her rush to exit the building to her awaiting carriage, her glass slipper was left behind. It was now with interest that Sherlock took up the enquiry of the missing glass slipper.

Without delay he sent a telegram to the young lady informing her that he would be happy to take up her case in the hope of reuniting her with the lost slipper. He asked her to join him at:
221b Baker Street, Marylebone, London so that he could discuss the finer details with her.

She was to arrive just as soon as was possible, so as not to lose any further time. Within thirty minutes a telegram was received, and the lady acknowledged his request and confirmed that she would arrive within the hour, she signed her name Princess Caroline.

Sherlock requested for some tea and cakes to be available from Mrs Hudson and to be served on their best china as he awaited the arrival of the distinguished guest. True to her word the Princess arrived in her carriage at precisely 3pm. Tea and cakes arrived as the Princess made herself comfortable. Sherlock enquired as to whether she had brought with her the slipper still on her possession, which she had. He took great care studying the glass slipper to look for any clues on either the sole or the heel.

Upon examination he found residue of a sticky substance, quickly reaching for his magnifying glass he was able to deduce that some sort of glue had been left as a residue on the slipper and that this had been the cause of the missing slipper to be lost. He asked the Princess for more details as she accepted a piece of Mrs Hudson's homemade cake. The Princess imparted that she had been in a rush to leave the ball the previous evening, due to an unfortunate argument that had erupted and in her haste had not noticed on the steps a shiny substance which caused the glass slipper to become dislodged from her left foot.

Not wishing to delay her exit another moment, she did not stop to retrieve the slipper, fully expecting one of the servants in attendance to reunite her with the slipper at a later hour.
Having waited unsuccessfully for its return the Princess thought she would contact Mr Holmes without delay. Sherlock was in agreeance and thanked her for her prompt action. He asked if he could retain the right slipper to assist him with his enquiries and the Princess agreed.

Upon her departure Holmes immediately grabbed his coat, his hat and his magnifying glass as a minute more was not to be wasted. He already had the address of where the ball had been held the previous evening and he must make haste before any clearing away of the evidence had been made. He hailed a cab to take him directly to Buckingham Palace.

Upon his arrival at the Palace, Holmes immediately began to look for the flight of stairs used by the Princess. Almost immediately he was pounced upon by the guards of the Palace. But once he explained who he was and why he was there, the guards escorted Holmes to the said staircase. Having brought with him his trusty magnifying glass he was able to examine every tread of the staircase. Upon examination, three steps from the bottom of the flight of stairs, there was the evidence he was looking for. A sticky residue with an unpleasant odour of fish. He deduced that this had to be a fish glue made from the species of fish called The Sturgeon. This type of glue was known to be used by Artists. Now it was just a case of getting access into the Palace to find where an Artist may have been working there.

The guard sought permission from his superiors and access was granted to Holmes to continue his search into the Palace. Once inside Holmes quickly followed his nose and was guided to an area closed off to staff by a large curtain. Behind the curtain the odour of fish glue was much stronger and led Holmes to an area of work being restored. There, on the table was a jar half full of the putrid smelling fish glue. He had found the evidence he had been seeking, now he needed to find the culprit and the missing glass slipper belonging to the Princess.

It was not long before Holmes had deduced that the restoration area had been abandoned, but on the floor underneath the table he noticed a small piece of paper.

Written on the reverse was an address. Could this be the address of the Artist's location? Tucking the small piece of paper into his overcoat pocket, Holmes retraced his steps through the Palace back to the flight of stairs. Looking again for any further clues, he spied upon some cream coloured brush hairs within the fish glue residue on the stair tread. He carefully removed the brush hairs and wrapped them in his own handkerchief and placed this into his overcoat pocket. He thanked the guards for their assistance and outside of the gates of Buckingham Palace he hailed a cab to take him to the address on the note paper he had found.

Holmes now found himself in Whitechapel, an area he was not unfamiliar with. The cab pulled away leaving Holmes to make his way to the premises. The building was of a commercial nature and a hive of activity. Withing minutes Holmes was able to find a willing soul to impart that one of the studios was let to an Artist. But that he had not shown up for work that day which was very much out of character for this man. Holmes tipped him a shilling as a thank you for the information and asked to be shown to the studio.

On entering the premises, Holmes immediately detected the smell of the fish glue in the air. Looking around for clues at the disarray in front of him, he could see that the Artist had hurriedly packed some belongings, but had left a very important belonging behind him, the missing glass slipper! There in plain sight for all to see this beautiful delicate glass slipper had been left behind. Quickly Holmes grabbed an old rag and wrapped this around the slipper before hiding the bundle inside his overcoat next to his chest for safe keeping and made a quick exit.

He hailed a cab and instructed the driver to take him to the residence of Princess Caroline. Upon his arrival he asked the staff for an audience with the Princess and of course giving his name, Sherlock Holmes. He was shown to a splendid room and asked to wait.

The Princess appeared almost immediately as Holmes started to unwrap the missing glass slipper from the Artists rag. The Princess was absolutely delighted that he had been able to locate and return the glass slipper to her. Holmes declared it was his pleasure to reunite her with the missing slipper and that he would send for her other slipper still held at 221b Baker Street, to be returned to her without delay. He remarked that it was one of the quickest cases he had been able to solve!

Before Holmes departed, he informed the Princess that she might like to have removed from her staff, the window cleaner in her employ, and whose window cleaning rag he was still holding in his hand, that had contained the glass slipper. It really was a case of, from a rag to riches.

Channeled through Paula from Sir Arthur Conan Doyle.

10. Nutrition Diploma

In the many healing sessions I have had the privilege of taking part in, I had noticed that due to the foods that people eat, many people are keeping themselves ill. I have learned over the years that our food is our medicine, and if you eat well your body will respond with wellness. The Psychic Surgeons give their healing to help people on many levels, but self-responsibility plays a major part of self-care after a healing session. I wanted to do more to help the people who came to see us, maybe offer some advice, but I wasn't qualified to do so.

Then, as if the Psychic Surgeons knew this, they gave me the 'nudge' I needed to get started. I kept seeing synchronicities to do with food, nutrition, the 5 a day advertisement reminders, and posters advocating to start drinking more water, eating more fruit and vegetables.

From this 'nudge' I started to research on the internet the different courses available on Nutrition. I found just what I was looking for with the Open College, a diploma in Health and Nutrition. It was an online course and there was a deadline of six months to complete it. All paperwork would be sent to me in the post and along with answering several test papers there was also a requirement to write a dissertation, oh my goodness. I know I'm not an academic and the thought of exams and a dissertation and at my age? What was I thinking? The thought of having to complete all of these requirements turned my tummy into worry.

The parcel arrived, there was a very large book to read and learn from before the exam papers could be answered. I set myself weekly targets to achieve and once I got into all the different subjects covered in the course, I really began to enjoy it. With revelations on food and its effects on the human body I was eager to learn more.

155

Having read and digested (excuse the pun) the information provided to me, I set aside the time to complete the exam papers and to write my dissertation, being very much aware that the deadline was looming before everything had to be returned for assessment.

I think three weeks passed by before the envelope was delivered in the post, a large hard backed A4 envelope, I wondered did this mean it contained a certificate? Had I passed? I held my breath as I opened the flap to the envelope and pulled the document out. I could see it read a Diploma in Health and Nutrition, my heart was racing, and as I completely pulled the certificate from the envelope, I could read the red writing "with Distinction". Tears filled my eyes, I could not believe it, me, Paula Jackson had got a diploma with distinction!

I never ever thought in my wildest dreams I would ever achieve something like this, tears ran down my face, as I then tried to read that I was now entitled to use these letters after my name…
Paula Jackson Dip. Health. N.

In my mind I said to the Psychic Surgeons "I've done it, I've got my diploma!" Now, if questioned I have a certificate to support my knowledge and advice. This pleased me to know that I will be able to help patients after a healing treatment with the Psychic Surgeons and give guidance, if needed, for their wellness. Plus this qualification will cover me if I should I travel to any different countries.

I have to say I have proudly framed my diploma certificate and it hangs on the wall where I can see it every day. It just goes to show you are never too old to achieve your dreams.
If you have something you have longed to achieve all I can say is, go for it. Preparation is everything and if you can do that, you too can achieve your heart's desire as I did.

11. We can't fix everything

This chapter has been channeled through Paula directly from the Psychic Surgeons.

"We the Psychic Surgeons are delighted to channel today through our beloved Paula we would wish to impart the reason for the title of this chapter."

"Healing comes in many forms, mentally, emotionally, physically, and spiritually. When a person is born they have chosen a path to follow in their lifetime. Often this is to experience the many complexities of the Soul and to experience balance in all things. This can often be to experience ill health, pain, emotional loss, physical hardship, which all sound extreme but are part of the Soul's path to expand through these experiences."

"At times, a patient's health condition has progressed too far, too far for the Psychic Surgeons to correct. We can often heal the condition but without clearing it from the mind or body of the patient. This means the active condition of the ailment is removed and the body is left to heal itself. Often the patient is left living with the condition that does not deteriorate any further.
There are times when the ailment has been detected in its early stages and can be healed for the condition to be removed completely."

"We the Psychic Surgeons know what is needed to help the patient to progress in life. Often it is a blockage that needs removing and once removed they can continue with their life journey. But other times there is more that needs to be cleared."

"We scan the mind and body to detect that which needs to be removed, cleared or healed. In many cases the mind is blocked, weighed down with the day to day worries of life."

"We can remove these mental blockages with either our distant or 1-2-1 healing through our beloved channel Paula who links us to the patients through her beautiful hands. The transference of energy through Paula reaches the patient to release, remove and return the balance to the mind."

"We the Psychic Surgeons know that all experiences have an emotion, and those that cut the deepest are retained and suppressed within the heart chakra, often by the individual just to allow them to get by in life. These emotions are the ones that can cause an imbalance within the individual, potentially causing illness to develop in the physical body. We release these suppressed emotions that no longer serve the individuals highest good and by doing so, this allows the person to move forward in life and allows their body to begin healing itself."

"The physical body carries out its own healing 24 hours a day, every day, every week, every year replacing cells, repairing the skin, renewing blood and rebalancing any organs that are in need of repair. Due to mental and emotional blockages these daily repairs cannot automatically be actioned by the body and that is when disease can manifest. By removing the mental and emotional blockages we the Psychic Surgeons can release these to allow the body to begin the self-healing process that it is designed to do."

"From the earliest time the body has been able to regenerate its cells to replenish the body to its optimum. Because of today's very busy lifestyle and the convenient and processed foods you now choose to eat on a regular basis, you are not giving your body the pure 'food medicine' it needs, and this too has a detrimental effect on the body and its ability to regenerate and heal itself daily."

"We the Psychic Surgeons find that due to the poor intake of balanced foods the body struggles with lower vibration foods, to energise itself for the processes it needs to carry out daily."

"So it is each individual person's responsibility to feed their body with more alkaline foods that will keep the body in balance. We have touched on this subject before in Paula s first book, but we find that people are still not looking after themselves as they are asked to do, and more illness is becoming evident because of this."

"Spiritually, we the Psychic Surgeons are aware of exactly where an individual should be in life. Where they should be in their spiritual connection with The Source. Many people have now discovered their psychic abilities and we are very pleased that those individuals are in touch with their true calling. Some people embrace it whilst others are worried and close the door to this wonderful connection with Spirit. A person's wellbeing can often be related to their spiritual wellbeing and we the Psychic Surgeons can clear spiritual blockages to allow the individual to continue on the spiritual path intended. During a healing session we can clear these blockages from the individual to release them to progress forward as has been planned. Each person is a whole and these elements, mental, emotional, physical, and spiritual make up the whole person and through the healing that we can offer, the individual is rebalanced again to proceed with their spiritual path."

"Fixing an individual is not impossible but we the Psychic Surgeons cannot exceed the boundaries of an arranged agreement made at birth, of the Soul's journey to experience all things in the individual's lifetime. Therefore we can only 'fix' what is permitted to allow the individual to proceed with life's planned experiences. We are here to assist in helping them to heal the areas that would otherwise 'block' their Soul's path. We rebalance the individuals Mind, Body and Soul so that when their life is at an end the passing into Spirit is balanced and the Soul's agreement is fulfilled."

"Trust that we the Psychic Surgeons are here to help in any way we can, always with the individual's permission to receive the healing that is right for them at the right time."

"Whilst we do all we can, it is often seen as not enough by the individual as their focus is only on the physical ailments and not on the other areas of wellbeing which we know to be out of balance. At times people perceive that the healing was 'no good' as it did not meet their expectation of being returned to wellness. Often, people have in their mind that they would wish for a 'miracle' to take place within the healing and for instant relief from pain and suffering be released. Whilst miracles do take place it is not for everyone to receive."

"As you will read in Paula's next chapter, she/we visited Lourdes in France a place of pilgrimage and miracles. We the Psychic Surgeons gave healing to the many people there through our beloved Paula's hands as she stood by the roadside. Many people were returned to wellness not knowing where the healing energy came from, only that they were indeed well again."

"So whilst we can't 'fix' everyone all of the time, we certainly can 'fix' a lot of the people all of the time. We will continue for many years yet to give healing through our beloved channel Paula helping those that need the healing energy we can provide."

"We are blessed to continue this wonderful work beyond our own years upon the earth plane, and through this divine connection with Paula, we continue our work to help as many people as we can."

"We thank you for your trust in us, the Psychic Surgeons, in the Psychic Surgeon healing we provide, and in the trust of our beloved channel Paula."

A channeled message from The Psychic Surgeons.

12. My Pilgrimage to Lourdes

I had received guidance back in September 2018 that I was to make a pilgrimage in the not too distant future. An overseas calling that would completely change my life! I wondered 'where' in the world I would be going. I had been given information that there would be healing in France for me, so I wondered if this was where I would be travelling to. It wasn't long before I received confirmation that yes, I would be travelling to France to experience a personal transformation, but where in France? I started doing some research on the internet of known spiritual areas, spiritual retreats and was delighted when an article on Lourdes appeared. Why didn't I think of that before? Of course, people travel to Lourdes for healing all the time and it was where miracles were performed or witnessed. I asked the Psychic Surgeons for their guidance and was excited when they indicated *"Yes,"* I was to travel to Lourdes for my pilgrimage.

I started to share with other people that this was where I would be travelling to. One beautiful message was given to me to say, "Paula you have worked hard, and this was your reward, Spirit trust you, you have earnt your right of passage and you will be initiated into The Council Realm of the Light at Lourdes." I knew that this pilgrimage would be special for me, but this was beyond anything I had thought might happen. They added, "Take a candle with you, take it with you to light with thanks, the candle should be emerald green in colour as Archangel Raphael is with you." Then another message was given to me, "The trip to France will exceed your expectations and you will spend five days at Lourdes, the weather will be good all the time." This was such useful information regarding the weather as Lourdes is in the foothills of the Pyrenees mountains, where the weather can turn cold or rain for days on end.

All that was left to do now was to book my flight and ask a dear friend if she would love to accompany me on my pilgrimage.

To my delight she accepted my invitation and together we planned when would be the best time to go. It was decided that July worked best for the both of us and we agreed the dates that allowed me to book my return flights. We started researching the hotels in Lourdes and Rhiannon, my friend, had two sets of criteria; the hotel must have a car park and it must have a swimming pool. Well, that was something I never thought of. But if this was on the list then I must search out a hotel that met these requirements. Within a few days we both came up with some hotel suggestions and narrowed it down very quickly to the one that stood out from all the rest. I think it won our vote not only on location within Lourdes and it's car park but because it had two swimming pools, one indoor and one outdoor, yay!

Monday 15th July arrived, my flight was on time and Rhiannon collected me from the French airport. I had a day of rest before our adventure began and I took advantage of the hot sunny weather to relax in her garden, to watch the many garden birds that visited the feeders and to listen to their birdsong. In my mind I wondered what lay in store for me on my pilgrimage, it was so exciting.

Wednesday 17th July 2019
My pilgrimage to Lourdes began with a road trip with my friend Rhiannon, who offered to drive us on the 4-hour drive from her home in the Charente region of France to Lourdes. We set off just after breakfast and planned to take a comfortable drive, stopping for some lunch, French bread and cheese (my favourite) and then continue leisurely until we arrived at Lourdes.
We arrived at our hotel at 4.30pm, unpacked and got ourselves ready to go out for our evening meal. In the middle of town, we found a lovely restaurant that overlooked the river with fabulous views of the Pyrenees mountains in the distance.

Rhiannon speaks lovely French, which puts me to shame, but the waiters in the restaurant spoke good English which helped me greatly. There was a lovely choice on the menu with quite a few dishes that I could have, being that I am vegetarian and in France they eat quite a lot of meat dishes. We even treated ourselves to a cocktail each to celebrate the start of our journey together.

After dinner we made our way through the streets of Lourdes and through the St Joseph Gate towards the beautiful Basilica of the Immaculate Conception, to watch the evening candlelight procession. This procession takes place every evening at 9pm. There were hundreds and hundreds of people lining the street as well as taking part in the procession. We walked up the ramparts of the Rosary Basilica to get a better view, to look down on the proceedings in the Esplanade. We could see the Pilgrims in the procession, many in wheelchairs and on stretchers with help from their Carers, Nurses or Nuns making their way towards where the Mass was taking place below us. Others walked along in the procession carrying a lighted candle.

(Part of the candle lit procession and photo of The Basilica)

As I watched my heart reached out to them all, such illness, I could feel myself getting emotional at what I was seeing. I just wanted to help. I felt guided that this was the right moment to connect to the Psychic Surgeons and bring them forward into my hands. I told them in my mind where I was in Lourdes and where I was standing, (as if they didn't already know!) Very gently my hands were moved as the Psychic Surgeons started scanning the crowds with my hands and fingers outstretched and they gave their healing to all. The healing did not interrupt the proceedings and I know the healing was received by those who needed it most.

A message had been given to me from a friend, "Your work is linked to this place, healing there will take thought, planning and care. But your journey will really start there to the work from above the skies I'm being told. Be confident but thoughtful, timing must be right."
I remember thinking this had been a very special evening; but more was to follow during the rest of my amazing pilgrimage.

Thursday 18th July
I had been guided that I needed to purchase a wooden cross from Lourdes during my stay. This was not something I had thought of purchasing but I would take notice of the guidance. I was to display the cross on my living room wall on my return home. I also needed a cross in the form of a piece of jewellery to wear on myself. Visiting several shops to purchase a wooden cross might sound quite easy to do, but there were many shops selling hundreds of wooden crosses. We walked around several but none of them felt right until we found the Roman Catholic Church shop. Although I am not Roman Catholic it seemed right to buy my wooden cross there. With many wooden crosses to choose from, my main guide helped me to choose the one I needed to purchase. My friend Rhiannon had been looking at the religious jewellery within the shop and spotted a small gold coloured bracelet that had a curved shaped cross that would rest upon my wrist.

164

I tried it on and although the shop assistant thought the bracelet was too small, I knew it was just the right size for the cross to stay in the correct position on my wrist without moving.

Having made my purchases the next thing we planned to do was a visit to the tourist information centre in Lourdes town centre, where we were drawn to book two tours, to visit the Chateaufort-Lourdes that towered above the town of Lourdes and the Funicular Railway that ran up the mountainside. We chose to do the Fort tour on the Thursday afternoon, learning all about the history of Lourdes and the Fortress itself. Then the Pic du Jer Funicular railway tour was booked to take place on the Saturday. After booking our tours we found the sweetest little Chocolate café and we treated ourselves to an indulgence of hot chocolate and a slice of their delicious chocolate cake, which was absolutely scrummy, she smiles.

That evening we got changed for dinner and took a stroll down the main street and found a new restaurant for our evening meal. This restaurant was also positioned alongside the river but this time our table was outside overlooking the water. We could hear the river flowing passed us and again there was a lovely selection of dishes to choose from on the menu. After dinner we then ventured into the town as the little shops were open late and bustling with people.

We returned to our hotel and sat in the Reception area and ordered some refreshments. Whilst sitting and chatting about our days' activities a gentleman came up to us and enquired had we stayed long in Lourdes and did we know that there was a musical show on in town? As the conversation (in French) continued, the gentleman informed Rhiannon that he was one of the producers of the show. It was all about the young life of St Bernadette the little girl who had seen eighteen apparitions of Our Lady of Lourdes the Virgin Mary.

He said the show was like a Broadway show and then proceeded to show us photographs of it from his mobile phone, it all looked very exciting. After he left us in Reception, we talked excitedly about going to the show. Should we go? Would we like to go? We both decided yes, we would go. Rhiannon found their website and we booked tickets for the following afternoon's performance. Totally unplanned but what a lovely treat for us and such a coincidence that the producer of the show should be staying in our hotel too!

Friday 19th July – My special day

This was the day I had been waiting for. Up and out early to arrive at the Lourdes Healing Baths for 8am. I had read that there would be long queues. The doors did not open until 9am and all the pilgrims were separated into Women only and Men only areas. The benches we sat on were comfortable and sheltered from the sun by a large wooden over hanging roof. (see photo) We waited in line for one hour whilst watching the Nuns and Helpers arrive, there were two Priests singing hymns in French to keep us all engaged whilst waiting, some people joined in with them.

Our turn finally came to enter the door to the healing baths. I felt excited inside of me because I knew that this was in fact my 'baptism' in the healing baths, just as the Psychic Surgeons had guided me. I was shown through to a curtained off area in a long corridor, where I took a seat and waited. Each lady including myself, was then asked in turn to enter into a curtained changing room, where Helpers assisted in the removal of all of my clothing whilst under a respectful gown to hide my nakedness. Then a white (damp) sheet was wrapped around my body and secured under my arm. I was now ready. There was a large cream coloured curtain hanging to the rear of the changing room, it was now time for the curtain to be drawn back. There in front of me was a sunken marble bath with three steps leading down into it, filled with the healing water.

There were Nuns and Helpers stood either side of the bath and they said a prayer for me before I then stepped down into the bath water. The water was freezing! Still wrapped in my white sheet; I was guided to walk through the water to the end of the bath and then asked to lower myself down into the water as if going to sit down on a chair. This I did and immediately the cold water covered my body right up to my neck and just as quickly as I had entered the water, so the many hands of the Helpers and Nuns were now lifting me out of it. All I can remember thinking in slow motion, in my mind was, oh my goodness me, how cold was that water? My mind did not have time to process that my body was now completely freezing cold. With my hands together in prayer position, I thanked the Nuns and Helpers for helping me. I was then asked to step out of the marble healing bath and return to the changing room where I dried myself off and dressed, again all discretely done for my privacy.

(Queues for the healing baths and the marble healing bath)

I made my way out through the exit door and into the sunshine, I tried to analyse how did I feel? Did I feel any different? I was expecting to, but I did not.

167

I waited in the sunshine for my friend Rhiannon to appear, she commented that it had been an emotional experience for her, and asked if I had felt anything? I had not felt any difference. We agreed that we both wanted to light a candle of gratitude. We made our way across the bridge over the river to the covered candle stations, where a donation was made for the candle we wished to purchase. I had been guided to choose a green coloured candle and was delighted when I saw a green tea light candle. I lit it from another burning candle and gave thanks as I did so.

It was now time to visit the healing water fountains that were located next to the Grotto, and to drink the beautiful healing water. There were no queues which was great and as I held my hands out under the flowing fountain I scooped the water into my hands and then into my mouth. The water had no taste but felt so fresh and cool. I did this several times each time giving thanks for the healing water I was receiving. I had now bathed in and had chosen to drink the healing water; I was cleansed inside and out!

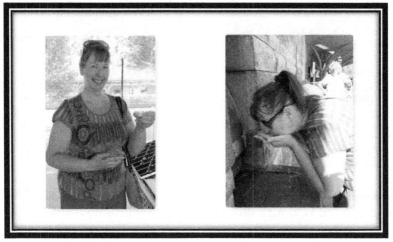

(My green tealight candle and then drinking the healing water)

Everything we had planned for the day was going so smoothly and I was now ready for the next very important element in my pilgrimage; a visit to the underground Basilica, which was known as The Basilica of Saint Pius X.

Already in possession of a map of the underground site, we found it hard to locate the entrance to this massive stadium; so in the end I had to ask at the book shop for directions. The entrance was next door and the most uninspired entrance for a Basilica. We started to descend on foot round and round like the spiral of a concrete multi storey carpark. We made our way down into the depths.

Once inside we waited for our eyes to acclimatize to the darkness, the sight that was before us was the most enormous concrete stadium, said to hold up to 25,000 people! It was not the prettiest building I've ever seen. In the centre of the stadium there was a Roman Catholic Mass taking place. Either side of the stadium were enormous banners hanging from the ceiling depicting images of many Saints.

Under these banners there was a walkway running along the outer edge of the stadium that, without intruding on the Mass taking place, one could walk around and towards the back of the stadium.
On the outer walls of the stadium were eighteen illuminated images of St Bernadette as she saw the eighteen different apparitions of Our Lady of Lourdes, Mother Mary. Two of these images are shown.

We continued along the long walkway towards the back of the stadium. I was looking for something special, a chair, a very special chair. The chair was where I was to be seated to receive my very special initiation from the Psychic Surgeons.

As we proceeded along the walkway, in the distance we could see all on its own, in the centre of a seating area a red velvet chair, there was no doubt about it, this was the chair! There was no one around, and the chair was not in a roped off area, so we walked over to it. I handed my bag and sunglasses to Rhiannon as she stepped back to observe at a distance what was about to take place.

I sat down in the red chair and placing my hands together in prayer position I connected to the Psychic Surgeons; they came forward into my hands. I asked them, "Was this the right place to be and was this the correct chair? "*Yes.*" I knew that on this day I was to receive my initiation from the Psychic Surgeons; after having had my baptism at the healing baths that morning. I was very excited and as the Psychic Surgeons gathered around me, they used my hands to carry out their ceremony.

My hands were lifted up into the air above my head by the Psychic Surgeons they then proceeded to pull white light down through the pyramid down into my Soul and into my heart. The new energy I experienced was immense. Then with my own hands they placed the white light onto my crown charka and then over my 3rd eye chakra. The Psychic Surgeons repeated this procedure twice. It felt so beautiful, unconditional love was bursting from my heart. I started to cry, they were tears of joy and emotional releasing. In my hands the Psychic Surgeons embraced me by placing my hands to my face. It truly was a beautiful moment. In total the initiation ceremony took approximately ten minutes to complete. My eyes were closed for the duration of the ceremony.

Without my knowing and whilst my initiation was taking place my friend Rhiannon, very discretely stood back and began to take some photographs of what was happening; knowing how special this moment was to me, she captured the images and also managed to take a short video too. These images I have kept private. But I have included two photographs, one of the red velvet chair I had sat in, and the other photograph of the modern metal statue of Christ that was in the centre of the stadium.

(The red velvet chair and the modern statue of Jesus on the cross)

Once the Psychic Surgeons had finished, I opened my eyes and just burst into tears. It was all so emotional for me. Rhiannon asked me if I was okay which I was, and I kept saying to her, I am fine really, but I couldn't stop crying, it was more releasing. After a few more minutes I finally composed myself, and we started to make our way back towards the entrance of the underground Basilica.

The midday Mass had finished, and the stadium was now emptying of people, so we walked to the centre of the stadium where there was a white table clothed alter, decorated with candles a wooden cross and flowers. There was a very modern interpretation of Jesus on the cross made in metal. We took some photographs, as you do, to remember such a special occasion. Finally, it was time to leave, and we made our way out into the sunshine, it was so bright after the darkness of the underground Basilica.

A much-needed lunch and refreshments were required to compose ourselves, so we made our way to one of the lovely side street restaurants for our lunch. We both remarked how special our day had been and how it really did exceed all of our expectations!

The next excursion that we had planned that day was to visit the upper levels of the beautiful Basilica of our Lady of the Rosary. It was not very far to walk from where we had lunch and we made our way down the walkways to the main Basilica where a Mass service was being conducted in German. We sat there for a while observing the architecture of this magnificent building and listening to the singing of the choir, but at 2.45pm we needed to leave; we had to catch the local bus as we had somewhere special to be.
The day just kept getting better as that afternoon we had booked our matinee tickets to the theatre to see the musical of Bernadette de Lourdes Le Spectacle Musical.

It was billed as a show of Broadway standards, plus we had met the producer of the show in our hotel reception, so we hoped that was the case. The show was magnificent, (all in French of course, but with subtitles on the side viewing screens). It was the story of the young girl Bernadette, on seeing the many apparitions of Mother Mary and then trying to convince everyone in the town what she had seen, the singing, the music it really was spectacular!

One song in particular resonated very deeply with me, it was called 'Why me?' and as she sang the song I could understand her words, her sentiment and why she was asking, of all the people in the world for this to happen to, why had she been chosen? Just like I had asked when I had been chosen by the Psychic Surgeons. It was very moving. We caught the bus back to our hotel and got changed for dinner. We chatted non-stop, what a wonderful special day we had had.

(Image of St Bernadette and the show's programme cover)

Saturday 20th July

Today was a sightseeing day. Entrance tickets had been purchased through the Tourist Board two days previously to take a ride on the Funicular Railway up to the top of the mountain that was situated just outside of Lourdes. Arriving at the station it wasn't long before the railway cars arrived, it took just eight minutes to get to the top with spectacular views on the way up.

Here we were at the top of the mountain and out into the fresh air. The sun was shining and straight away I spotted one of the Lourdes photo opportunity, of the 'heart'. We had already spotted quite a few of these hearts dotted around Lourdes town, so we just had to take a photo of ourselves and the fantastic views in the background. I took photographs of rapture birds flying overhead and circling in the thermals, more photos of the fantastic views and the railway cars and then it was time to visit the bat caves.

There was a tour of approximately forty-five minutes taking visitors through the caves of stalagmites and stalactites but with the added bonus of seeing the bats who were resident in the caves. Blankets were provided for us to wrap ourselves in as it was quite cold in the caves as we followed the guide. We did manage to see a few of the bats flying over our heads as we disturbed them on the tour, but they were too quick for us to photograph. At the exit door of the tour, there was the opportunity to walk up to the summit of the mountain. Although the path was just a dirt track, Rhiannon and I decided we wanted to take a leisurely climb and after about twenty minutes we finally made it to the top. Just in time to see a helicopter flying below us, which was really odd to see as we were so high up. There were some beautiful little wildflowers growing in every nook and crevice and I wondered how they survived when winter came along. All day long we had a song worming its way through our brain, Funiculi' Funicular' la la la la la, an old Italian song which really was written about a Funicular railway!

As we took our refreshments that afternoon, we started to sing the song, oh how we laughed, it seemed that at every opportunity we would be reminded of this song all the way through our days in Lourdes. Even on my return home to the UK the song still seemed to crop up reminding me of this lovely day.

On our return to the hotel we decided it was time to use the heated outdoor pool. The weather in Lourdes was lovely and hot and after our expedition up the mountain this was just what was needed, the only shock was, the pool wasn't heated. Oh my goodness me. It was so cold compared to the heat of the day. Almost as quickly as we got in, we got out; she laughs. But now brave enough to take another dip we swim for a good half an hour. It was time to get ready for dinner and explore another part of Lourdes town centre and another new restaurant we had not been to before. All the fresh air of the day, being at the top of the mountain soon took its toll and an early night was beckoning.

Sunday 21ˢᵗ July

This was our last full day in Lourdes and after breakfast we planned to find the walk called 'The Way of the Cross'. On the map it showed we needed to start the walk at the Basilica.

We began following the directions and soon we could see the Angel statue signpost pointing the way for us to follow. The walkway was steep as it curved its way up the hillside, but wonderful views could be seen below.

The Way of the Cross depicts the crucifixion of Jesus Christ in fourteen different bronze statue scenes, which were placed very respectfully along the climbing pathway up a hillside. After climbing up the mountain top the day before I wasn't expecting to be climbing up yet another hill again so soon! My poor legs.

At each set of statues, we took time to sit and view and take in the scene before us. I took photographs to follow the story and as we turned the corner we could see Jesus on the cross, it was very emotional to see. The path winded and twisted up the hill side and the final scene was when Jesus had risen, and the stone was rolled away. It was very respectfully done and something I am so pleased to have seen. On our way down, we were able to stop at a water fountain to refresh ourselves in the heat of the day, and it was very welcome.

When we returned to our hotel to have a quiet five minutes before getting ready for dinner, I connected to Spirit, to my own main guide who gave me a message…to say, "I was needed, to send some healing that evening with the Psychic Surgeons. I would be informed where and when."

After dinner I was guided to return to the evening candlelit procession which took place at 9pm, but this time I was to stand beside the avenue of Pilgrims as they passed by to make their way to the Esplanade for blessings and Mass. That day I had received a text message to say, "Spirit is rewarding you for your service, you have been chosen from millions, just be in the moment let it flow." Just as I was guided to do, Rhiannon and I made our way to the Basilica of the Immaculate Conception. We were early, arriving around 8.30pm so we took a seat on the benches and people watched, whilst waiting for the candle lit procession to arrive.

After a little while it felt like I was being 'pushed' to get up. So I made my way to take position at the side of the procession avenue, as I had been guided to do. I could see in the distance the hundreds of people in the procession were coming towards me.

The candle lit procession was led by volunteers carrying the statue of Our Lady of Lourdes, the Virgin Mary, followed by many Priests and Nuns and then the hundreds of Pilgrims. Many were carrying their lighted candles and singing 'Ave Maria' a hymn that was sung every day whilst we were at Lourdes.

As the procession neared, I asked the Psychic Surgeons to come forward into my hands, the energy felt very strong in my fingers and hands that evening. I had no idea just how many of the 55 Psychic Surgeons in the Team were coming forward to give their healing that evening through my hands, all I knew was that we had a big task ahead of us.

Then, as the procession of Pilgrims started to file passed me the Psychic Surgeons began to move my hands. My palms facing out towards the people as they walked towards me. The Psychic Surgeons started giving the healing to all those in need. My hands were throbbing with the energy flowing through me, I must have been standing there for over half an hour just sending the healing out, whilst people filed passed me. Sometimes I caught the eye of people and smiled at them and they smiled back at me. Others looked bewildered at my healing hands being stretched out towards them. Words cannot express to you the emotion that welled up inside of me, helping so many people but all at once. It was so beautiful and overwhelming at the same time.

Only after everyone had filed passed me, did I get given the push again to step out into the now empty avenue and stand there, with my hands scanning over the whole crowd of people in front of me. The Psychic Surgeons were sending healing to everyone. It was amazing!

After the healing had been sent, I asked the Psychic Surgeons if lots of people had received the healing? They replied, "*Yes, enough to make a difference.*"

Without me knowing, my friend Rhiannon had been taking photographs of me as the healing was being sent out through my hands. These photographs show me standing in front of the Basilica where the evening Mass was taking place and standing at the side of the avenue with my hands containing the Psychic Surgeons, outstretched sending healing towards the Pilgrims.

After the Psychic Surgeons had left my hands, Rhiannon and I made our way to the Grotto. We had been recommended to attend the evening service there, to feel the emotions of this wonderful place and to pay our respects to the Virgin Mary and just 'be' in the moment. We queued to file passed her statue. There was a Mass taking place, people were seated, many candles were lit. It was a moment to treasure. Afterwards we felt drawn to light our own candle of thanks.

We took loads more photographs as everything looked so serene in the evening light, even the Basilica was illuminated and looked very striking, high up on the hill above us. We had just finished taking out photos when all of a sudden, the lights directed towards the Basilica where turned off for the evening. Talk about perfect timing. We continued to walk amongst the Pilgrims as we began making our way back to our hotel.

Then, just before I went to bed that night, I received a text message, the message was relayed from Spirit to say, "Today was the most powerful day for you, all went to plan." It was wonderful to receive this confirmation.

Monday 22nd July

Having checked out of our hotel we had the morning to ourselves before setting off on our journey home. We chose to return to the area around the Basilica because that's where the Musée des Miraculés (Museum of the Miraculously Healed) was located. Being a Healer myself I wanted to see what miracles had taken place in Lourdes since 1858 and I was excited to see what the museum had in store. As we entered the building, we saw the exhibition was located on the first floor. The exhibition room was long and well-lit and around each of the four walls were the many pictures of the people who had been acknowledged as having received a miracle from the healing waters of Lourdes.

Of course everything was in French, which was very frustrating for me, but Rhiannon came to my rescue and translated as much as she could about each person's medical condition and how the miraculous cure had taken place, either during or after their visit to Lourdes. We took our time and stopped at all of the seventy pictures. There were many different medical conditions recorded as miracles for illnesses and conditions such as blindness, paralysis, tuberculosis, heart diseases, ulcers, abscesses, arthritis, and cancer. To be able to understand this was very important to me, and I was so grateful to Rhiannon for helping me.

It has been acknowledged by the selected Medical Bureau of Lourdes that there are in fact only seventy actual miracles that have been officially recognised as having taken place since 1858 to this present day. Where people have been 'cured' beyond scientific explanation. There have been many thousands of other cases presented to the Medical Bureau where people have claimed to have been cured, but their cases have not been accepted. The museum puts arguments forward both for and against the miracle claims as many people are still sceptical of the healing powers of the water at Lourdes.

Located down the centre of the exhibition room were floor standing banners of approximately six feet in height, some were depicting images of the Basilica of the Immaculate Conception at Lourdes, and others depicted Our Lady of Lourdes, the Virgin Mary.

I found myself standing in front of another banner with the images of four Doctors on it. Again, everything on the banner was in French, but what stood out to me was that one of the Doctor's was responsible for the setting up of the Office of Medical Observations from 1883-1891. My curiosity got the better of me and whilst standing in front of the Doctors banner, I asked for the Psychic Surgeons to come forward into my hands. I explained to them that I was standing in front of this banner with the four Doctors images on and would the Psychic Surgeons be able to confirm to me please if, any of these four Doctors were connected to, or are part of the Psychic Surgeon Team? "*Yes*" was the reply. (I knew it!) I then asked, "May I know how many Doctors from this banner are in the Psychic Surgeons Team, is it one, two, three or four?" "*One*" was their reply. I then asked, "If I read out the names of each of the Doctors, please would you indicate through my hands which Doctor it is?" "*Yes.*" I read out each name and when I finally reached Doctor number 4 the Psychic Surgeons moved my hands and replied "*Yes.*" The Doctor they had chosen was Doctor Dunot of Saint-Maclou, who had set up the Office of Observations. OMG! One of the Psychic Surgeons who now works through my hands was once here in Lourdes!

The synchronicity of this was not lost on me and I called my friend Rhiannon over to explain to her what had happened and pointed out the Doctor that was now part of the Psychic Surgeons Team.
Not only was my journey to Lourdes for my own personal pilgrimage, for my initiation, and for healing to the Pilgrims, but it was also an acknowledgement of the eminent Doctor who had now joined the Psychic Surgeon Team.

How incredible is that? I really am so lucky to have such wonderful Surgeons and Doctors working through me to give the healing to so many.

We left the Miracles exhibition on such a high and made our way back to the hotel to collect the car. It was a lovely sunny day, and we had a four-hour journey ahead of us to return home. There was no rush, and we would enjoy the views of the French countryside on our way, especially the many fields of sunflowers with their sunny faces almost waving at us as we passed by.

I can honestly say 'my cup runneth over', this wonderful spiritual journey really did exceed all of my expectations just as I had been told it would.

13. A Poem for Paula

The Surgeons saw the suffering on the earth plane they had left
But longing still to practice they began to feel bereft
For they had advanced knowledge which they longed to use and share
As on the earth man hadn't yet the skills that they'd learnt there

So they had lots of gatherings and pondered what to do
For there must be a solution to make their dreams come true
They had to find a method to reach and help on earth
Determined, persevering their ideas were taking birth

After many years of searching for a woman or a man
They finally found Paula and their time with her began
At last we've found her, she's the channel that we need
We've searched the whole world over for our mission to succeed

Excitement filled the heavens as the group of Surgeons met
Now Paula was discovered all their mission plans were set
They'd found their perfect channel now through her they could reveal
Their skill and advanced knowledge where there was a need to heal

A natural receiver, she was honest, pure, and kind
She was the perfect vessel just the sort they had in mind
They'd paved the way to train her, though Paula had no idea
That Psychic Surgeons plans for her were drawing very near

She was led to Spiritual healing, was advancing every day
They guided and directed as she travelled on her way
They monitored her progress till she understood and knew
Her hands were lifted in the air for the work she had to do

She'd follow their directions as her graceful hands were raised
Her fingers floating over where the suffering was erased
The Surgeons revealed problems often starting in the mind
And with progressive healing many cures they were to find

The time of treatment varied, but easement and peace retrieved
As many symptoms disappeared and pain would be relieved
So now they work together, such a joyful healing Team
For Paula and the Psychic Surgeons have all achieved their dream.

By Chrissy Greenslade, Poet.

14. The Lockdowns

My last one-to-one clinic of 2020 was held on Saturday 14th March, when I attended one of my lovely healing day clinics in Christchurch, Dorset. It was a busy, fully booked day offering the healing from the Psychic Surgeons to the people who had booked to receive their psychic surgeon healing. It was lovely to see familiar faces, catch up on all the news and we had a few laughs too. Little did I know then that it was to be the last I would see of these friendly faces for an awfully long time.

When the lockdown was officially announced my initial thoughts were one of concern. For the services that we offer to people, were, like many others going to be affected. All external events that I had booked in the diary to attend; were cancelled. All my monthly clinics were closed due to the government restrictions. All that was left for me to offer to people was the Psychic Surgeons Distant Healing. Was that going to be enough? Would I have enough income to live off? I talked to the Psychic Surgeons I asked them for their guidance. They reassured me we would be alright, and I was not to worry. Easier said than done, but as the weeks passed more and more people contacted me as they realised that they couldn't get to see me to receive the one to one healing from the Psychic Surgeons. In particular needing help with their mental health and wellbeing as people struggled with the confinements of the lockdown. To say I was thrilled and relieved at the same time was an understatement. The Psychic Surgeons were bringing to me the people that needed their healing, they were just so amazing!

As I had worked from home before and enjoy my own company, my confinement did not feel too different to cope with. I was safe, secure, warm, had food on my table and most importantly I was healthy. The weeks passed; we were permitted daily outside exercise of one hour. I used this time every day to walk through the playing fields near to where I live.

The sun came out all through March, April and into May and it was a joy to feel the warmth of the sun on my face each day, although when it rained, I stayed indoors.

Living in a totally secure environment at home for many weeks, my balanced energy and vibration played an important part in my daily wellbeing. It became more and more noticeable as the first lockdown continued that going outside was becoming an issue for me. Not that I suffer with agoraphobia, I don't, it was just the thought of the possible contamination mixing with others. At this point it was not mandatory to wear face masks. I made myself a routine of going food shopping to the supermarket once every two weeks. Each time I arrived at the supermarket there seemed to be a different system in place, a different route to take to enter the store. Already I felt like I was floundering. Arrows everywhere, follow this one, follow that one. The shopping trolleys were not accessible until I reached the store entrance door, then realised I was holding up the queue as I struggled to quickly release the trolley from its chain.

Aware now that social distancing came into force even more strictly around the supermarket, my eyes were everywhere, who was walking towards me, were they too close? Who was coming up behind me? Overtaking me too closely and all this was happening before I had even entered the main shopping area. I had my shopping list of items to purchase and knowing the store layout well, started to make my way to the fresh fruit and veg, only to find I was going the wrong way! I was walking against the flow of people and I'm not following the floor marked arrows. Making a hasty retreat to correct my error I walked down several aisles I did not need to visit to get into the flow of where I needed to be.

But goodness me, people were hindering my path, stopping in the middle of the aisle instead of to the side, pondering over their purchases, standing right in front of the items I wanted to buy and people overtaking me very closely, too closely.

A couple of times I had to ask people to give me room please, which I am pleased to say they did. Looking at my shopping list there were only a couple more items to purchase and then I was on the home run to the checkout. I felt exhausted, this was not like me, I'm never bothered by crowds or for that matter going food shopping, but this was different, I could feel myself getting anxious.

At last, I was in sight of the checkout I just needed to queue at a distance and wait my turn. Everyone seemed to want to walk around me. They were so close, where was the observing of social distancing? I found myself holding my breath as they walked past me. Thank goodness, it was now my turn to unload my shopping onto the conveyor belt, pay the checkout lady and be on my way.

Having brought my shopping bags into my home, I took off my jacket and washed my hands. I proceeded to clean and put away my shopping into the cupboards and then again washed my hands. It was now time for a well-earned cup of tea. As I sat down on the sofa, I was aware that both my hands were red hot. Really hot with so much heat coming from the palms of my hands! This is always the sign to me that the Psychic Surgeons are in my hands. Odd, because I had not called them forward that day, yet they were there waiting for me. I put down my cup of tea and greeted them with my hands in the prayer position. I realised that they were waiting to cleanse and clear me, they knew I had been outside and that my Aura, energies and vibration had been contaminated by other energies from my outing. Straight away the Psychic Surgeons moved my hands to clear and wipe away the anxiety and unwanted energies I might have picked up. It took them several minutes until they were satisfied that I was back in balance.

I thanked them so much for looking after me and said goodbye to them as they departed. The heat from my hands disappeared and were now back to normal temperature.

As I leaned back on the sofa with my cup of tea, I sat in gratitude at how lucky I am to have the wonderful Psychic Surgeons looking after me and looking after my wellness. They were looking after their channel, that's me. I am truly blessed.

As the weeks passed my interaction on the internet and social media increased, as it did for many others. I loved seeing what other people were up to, how were they filling their lockdown days? Lots of photographs of nature from daily walks appeared. Lots of food pictures from baking cakes and pies and photos of their pets too. Funny, laugh out loud videos started to appear, and the humorous antics that people got up to. A good laugh was just what I needed. Then invitations starting arriving in my inbox to join online groups for meditations, live readings and online sound bath events etc. How innovative of people using social media as an outlet for their business and for their hobbies. How could I be part of that? How could we offer the Psychic Surgeons healing to the many people that needed it in these difficult times?

In April I was invited to take part in an online group healing event, where a group of healers including myself, sent out healing to the world. It was a very emotional experience to be part of and something that I dearly wanted to do again. Of course this was the 'nudge' from Spirit that I needed to get going.

A couple of days later whilst taking my shower, thoughts were coming into my mind. You could do this; you don't need anyone you can do this by yourself. The thoughts continued in my mind as I got dressed. I grabbed a pen and paper and started taking notes of what to do.

Within a couple of hours I had set up an online event called 'The Psychic Surgeons Distant Healing Event' to take place on Friday 17th April at 11am.

It was to be a fifteen-minute distant healing session for anyone who would like to put their name down to receive the Psychic Surgeons healing. I had asked the Psychic Surgeons for their guidance and if this was okay to put this event in place? They were so excited that they gave me an extra squeeze, and I can imagine them thinking, at last, she's got it! (She laughs).

Excitedly I put the event onto all three of my social media pages and straight away got lots of 'likes', and 'I'm interested' in attending and 'I'm going' confirmations. People started adding their names and those of family, friends and lost loved ones to the event. I was thrilled. To acknowledge each person's healing request, I 'liked' their post, so they knew I had seen it. Very kindly people 'shared' the event so that more and more people could be included in receiving the distant healing.

Then the thought struck me, was there a limit to the number of people who could take part in the event to receive the healing? After all there was only me, the Psychic Surgeons channel. I only have one pair of hands, I needed to seek their guidance and immediately connected to the Psychic Surgeons. I always ask the Psychic Surgeons for their guidance with a series of questions,
"Was there a limit to the number of people that the Psychic Surgeons could send their distant healing to?" "*No, there was no limit.*" Wow! This then prompted me to ask another question,
"Could the Psychic Surgeons send the healing to hundreds of people all at the same time?" "*Yes, we can.*"
I then asked,
"Could you send the healing to more than one thousand people all at the same time?" "*Yes, we can.*"
I sat there trying to digest what they had told me; I was in awe at the ability that the Psychic Surgeons have to send the distant healing to so many people all at the same time!

I then asked the question,
"Will all of the 55 Psychic Surgeons in the Team be coming forward to give their healing for our event?" "*Yes, ALL the Psychic Surgeons together with the Healing Angels would be coming forward to give the distant healing.*"
"Through my one pair of hands?" "*Yes.*"

It's a lot of information for one person to take in. How? How do 55 Psychic Surgeons squeeze their energy through my hands? Of course they don't actually do that (I think) but once the connection is made, they work and connect to the people through me. How exciting was this? I couldn't wait for the Friday event to arrive. There had been an amazing response to the event and nearly 100 people had put their names down to receive the Psychic Surgeons Distant Healing.

On the Friday morning just before we began the event, I said a prayer and asked for our event to be blessed and for all the people to receive the distant healing. Tears began to stream down my face, I knew they were not my tears, but this overwhelming feeling of unconditional love descended around me, it was beautiful. At five minutes to eleven I connected to the Psychic Surgeons and asked them were they ready? "*Yes.*" I asked, are the Angels with us? "*Yes.*" At 11am I was guided to click on and use the event page advertisement using my laptop and through this the Psychic Surgeons would connect to every single person who had put their names down and asked for the healing.

It took exactly fifteen minutes to send the distant healing and at 11.15am we finished. There had been no massive surge of energy through my hands as I had been expecting from ALL of the Psychic Surgeons in the Team, they were so gentle with me, just moving my hands as they do with every distant healing we send out. For me, this healing event had felt exactly the same as an individual distant healing session.

I thanked the Psychic Surgeons and the healing Angels for coming forward to give the healing. I then posted on my social media pages that we had finished and that the Distant Healing had been sent out that morning from the Psychic Surgeons. I thanked everyone for participating that day, to drink their water and I detailed how they may now feel after the healing session...

*More calm *Tearful *Energised *More positive *Seeing colours *Tingles *Happy *and a feeling of unconditional love.

I asked; please let me have your feedback on anything you may have felt during the session, because the Psychic Surgeons have guided me that we are going to do the distant healing event again this time next week.

Having asked for feedback from everyone, I could not have imagined the response I was about to receive. I was inundated with wonderful replies from people feeling the Psychic Surgeons distant healing, actually feeling the Psychic Surgeons in or on their body, seeing colours, seeing the Surgeons faces, feeling the energies, people being moved to tears, people being physically moved by the Psychic Surgeons. For me, it was overwhelming, I felt really emotional as I read one comment after the other. Tears streamed down my face at the realisation of how many people had felt the amazing distant healing from the Psychic Surgeons. How incredible was this? We had just sent distant healing to one hundred people living hundreds of miles away from each other and each of them felt the Psychic Surgeons distant healing. There was even a lady in Canada who had requested the distant healing, although she would be fast asleep in her bed due to the time difference, she still felt the distant healing and awoke feeling revived refreshed and with a sense of calm.

191

Just as the Psychic Surgeons had guided me to do, I set up another event for the following week for Friday 24th April at 11am.

Again, I added the event to my three social media pages and asked people to add their names. This time the response to the event was unbelievable! There were nearly 250 names added to the event.

On the day just as we had done before, we sent out the distant healing to everyone who put their names down. Again, I asked people for their response and feedback from the distant healing they had received, the public replies that came back were even more incredible.

Relief of physical pain, a lightness of mind, a releasing of emotions, the comments just kept coming in. I replied to each and every one of them to acknowledge that I had read their reply. To my amazement the Psychic Surgeons indicated that we would be doing another distant healing event the following Friday, 1st May at 11am.

We continued to offer the distant healing event each week for nine weeks throughout the first lockdown, helping people who had needed the healing whether for physical ailments or for mental health or emotional wellbeing. It had been a delight for me to help so many people.

I now realise that this 'special gift' that I have been given, has been given to me for more than just one-to-one individual healings at a time. And through these weekly distant healing events, with ever growing numbers of people receiving the distant healing, it has shown me just what can be achieved by the Psychic Surgeons. As their channel they do test me, these series of weekly events had pushed me beyond my comfort zone, putting myself out there even more, to show more people what the Psychic Surgeons can do.

As the weeks turned to months and the months turned to Summer with glorious warm sunshine, we all felt so much better.

The virus had not gone away but had been reduced greatly to allow us to start meeting up again with family and friends.

For some people they were able to return to the office for work and shops began opening their doors again. I excitedly asked the Psychic Surgeons would we be returning to the Mind, Body Spirit events that had been previously booked in the diary, cancelled or postponed? *"No."* was their reply. Would I be returning to my monthly clinics? *"No."* I was shocked, no. But why not? After many questions to the Psychic Surgeons and seeking their guidance I received my answer. I was to remain at home for the foreseeable future offering the distant healing. Little did I know that we were to enter into a second and third lockdown, but the Psychic Surgeons knew!

So, as I was guided to do, I remained working from home sending out the distant healing to the many, many people who booked an appointment with us. But there was also more to this request from the Psychic Surgeons, they wanted me to bring something new to people. I spent many hours on the internet researching as they had guided me. I share more about this later in my book.

But as Summer turned to Autumn it became more evident that we were to enter into a second lockdown and on the 5th of November 2020 a one month lockdown began in England. I asked the Psychic Surgeons could we be of help to people again sending out the distant healing on the social media events as we had done earlier in the year? *"Yes."* So it was with great pleasure that I announced we were going to be offering the distant healing again. People signed up adding their names as requested to each event that took place. Many people were relieved we were able to help them again by offering the distant healing to everyone. Over the second lockdown we were able to set up four weekly distant healing events to help people get through the challenging times. Again, I received so many "thank you's" from people, with their public feedback from their experiences of the healing they had received from the amazing Psychic Surgeons. We were so happy to help.

15. Messages after the Healing

These are some of the incredible 'Messages after the Healing' that I received from the participants of our weekly social media distant healing events. I was guided by the Psychic Surgeons that we needed to share these comments for people to read, as we helped so many people especially with their mental health during and after the difficult times of the Lockdowns. I have also included some feedback comments from people who have received a one-to-one healing from the Psychic Surgeons, and feedback from individual distant healing sessions with the Psychic Surgeons.

~ ~ ~ ~ ~ ~

* "I'm a different person from the first healing, I even walked from my bedroom to my bathroom this morning without my walking stick! I'm energised in my head as well, and waking up with ideas, and motivation. Thank you."

* "Thank you so much, very vivid today, lots going on, felt healing in my head, chest, tummy, and lower back. Feel much lighter and clearer now, bit of a headache so drinking plenty of water. Thank you again and thank you for being there."

* "I felt lots of work around my solar plexus which isn't a surprise. Also my spine which is still tingling wonderfully. Thank you."

* "At the start of the healing I felt a presence and said "namaste", my arms were moved around. I am sure my back has improved, thank you. You are a lovely lady with a heart of gold I can see why the Psychic Surgeons chose you to work through."

* "I felt a lot happening, at first in my head then my eyes, I felt work happening there, different for each eye. Moving to feelings like waves over my heart, and then more focused around my heart. There was a general heightened energy in all my cells, like a tiny buzzing or tingling."

* "After yesterday's distant healing session, I woke this morning and the most amazing thing happened. The Psychic Surgeons worked on my gums yesterday but continued to work on a loose back tooth during the night! I kept waking up and feeling my tooth moving about like it was being pulled. When I woke up this morning my tooth fell out cleanly, no pain, no blood. I haven't been able to get to my dentist because of lockdown to have it treated, and my hospital consultant was very concerned about the risk of infection. I am absolutely delighted that this has happened, and I don't have to worry anymore, many, many, many thank you's."

* "I am feeling very relaxed. I saw what looked like a ribbon tightly tied around a part of my brain and untie itself! Very interesting."

* "I first felt light pain in my upper back, then in my chest, and on the right side of my chest and abdomen together with slight fluctuations. The healing then went to my centre breastbone. Then the same feelings in my upper stomach and a slight sensation to lower stomach."

* "I could feel 'warmth' in the areas that were being worked on. It is interesting that the Surgeons worked on my womb and my hormones to rebalance these. Hopefully, this will now benefit me with the constant bleeding I have been experiencing for so many months. (And it did!)"

* "My husband has asked me to say that he has had a marked reduction in anxiety since his distant healing session with you and the pain in his neck was notably reduced immediately after his healing session and disappeared completely within a day or two after!"

* "Thank you, definitely tingling in my mind! I felt aching in my SI joint (sacroiliac joint) on the left and some brief pressure around my throat area."

* "Here is my experience. It started with violet light pulsing into my third eye and then energy sensations flowing into my Solar Plexus. Then pulsating light flowing into me. I felt some movements in my lower back and then Whoosh - I couldn't stop crying on and off for about five minutes. Someone (the Nurse) was holding my hand and sending so much love and compassion that it made me cry more! Then the work began on my body as you described. I felt they were also trying to lengthen my right leg to correct the pelvis. Just at the end I actually saw a face of a Surgeon! Thank you and the Surgeons for such an amazing healing."

* "My Physiotherapist was amazed at how much easier the movements in my neck were considering that I had not seen her for over a month! Halfway through the healing session and for no apparent reason something made me do a brief exercise I had been given, to moving my head from side to side. The pain in my knees is certainly easier and the neck and left shoulder not as painful. Thank you."

* "Thank you, so much dear Paula, for everything, your feedback was SO accurate! I could feel the Psychic Surgeons working on the areas you told me about, especially on the heart and the womb. I feel lighter in my head and wanting to laugh!"

* "I had extensive work done on my head/brain. I could feel pulsating sensation in it. Also they worked with my lower back, hips, and spine alignment. Furthermore the Surgeons worked with both leg calf muscles and tendons. Interestingly I could feel the different points on my body as a bearable pain sensation. After that I fell into a deep sleep... Thank you for all you do."

* "I have to say my mental stress has greatly lessened since your healing and I am more positive. I feel much better now and have not had the depression since."

* "I feel just this deep calmness and the pain of the sciatic nerve has gone. I still feel very peaceful and have no pain."

* "Much praise to your wonderful Surgeons. Felt pressure on my chest, someone touched my left toe and elbow. My hands felt like they were pulsating and were sinking through the floor! Felt as light as a feather. Warmth across my forehead. Saw lots of purples and greens. I noticed a couple of your Surgeons have huge hands! I also saw a brief glimpse of a Doctor with a white beard wearing a brown suit. I heard his voice say, *"Well done for sitting still"* lol. It was much appreciated, and I think it is lovely what you are doing."

* "Thank you for the healing, there were two male Surgeons working on myself, one in front and one behind also a nurse in a blue uniform came in and I felt an amazing energy."

* "I actually like to have your book open on the picture page of the Surgeons when having my healing session. Your book is so enlightening on your wonderful journey, thank you."

* "I sensed them working on my mental state and my uterus especially. Thanks for informing me of what they worked on. I will certainly leave you a feedback, your work is amazing! Thank you for being on Earth and being so connected, it's a true gift."

* "Wow! That was very powerful, with a sensation of long, grey twisted ropes being pulled out of me! Felt uplifting and motivating energy today. Feel like I'm so much more smilier!"

* "At the end I knew I had two of your Surgeons with me, but I don't know which ones ... I thanked them and felt the peace ... wonderful."

* "I felt cords being pulled from my solar plexus and my hands were on fire, still tingling. Amazing experience. Very grateful."

* "That was wonderful! I could really feel them working in my heart. I had visions of clouds of dark smoke which gradually got lighter and went white. Then an image of dark strings of emotion that connected me to the past all being gathered up, then cut through. Then my heart was filled with love and light, and I was given a long hug, and heard that I can do that for myself at any time I like. It was so lovely. I smelt a musty sort of smell, sort of like old books from an old place at times today, during some healing they did on my head. So interesting your feedback on my digestive system - I haven't been eating enough fruit and been eating too many crisps. I have been drinking lots of water though and will keep that up. Thank you, Paula, thank you Surgeons."

* "My granddaughter could feel the energies, twitching felt as well in her kidneys, which were sore before, then they stopped hurting and her back feels better."

* "Once I relaxed, I could see their faces, fantastic, thank you. I think four, maybe a couple more, they were quite quick, and I found it very comforting, they came in one after the other."

* "I connected with you at the specified time and definitely had some work done on my neck as there was some cracking sounds from my neck as a couple of bones seemed to be put back into place. Didn't know they were out! But felt much better afterwards, although a little spacey for a few minutes. Thanks again to you and the Surgeons."
* "I now feel more positive, more relaxed & generally my body feels good...the aches & pains in the lower back & kidneys have gone! Thank you. Much love to you all."

* "I feel so relaxed.... during the session I felt pressure in my 3rd eye area, my temples and jaw. I was laid with my hands on my belly, and it felt as if hands were on top of my hands! Again a beautiful experience. Much gratitude lovely lady!"

* "I felt a cool energy on my left side of my body it felt serene and helped me relax. I was then asked to put my hands in prayer position which I did. They then went to a spot between the left side of my neck and shoulder and was doing something there for a good five to ten minutes felt pressure there. Then I felt someone place a cool energy on my left side of my face and forehead which felt gentle. They continued to use their energy on my left side of face and forehead. Lastly, they placed their hands on my shoulders and I felt a lovely warm energy like I was being hugged. Thank you so much for your healing I really appreciated it."

* "That was incredible! My body physically was moved in so many ways. I said to myself this morning that I miss my Chiropractor, but I don't need her now! Many thanks. It really was fantastic Paula. My body was moved back into place - whatever place they wanted me to be in. Bless them it took them a long time - 50 minutes! I had a guided meditation afterwards and my hand gave a movement by itself!"

* "Can't believe all this happened in 15minutes!! Healing to different parts of my body by several different beings, and a family reunion. Wow! Mind blowing."

* "It was very interesting. I felt the energy come into my abdomen area like a flooding. Work continued across my lower back, hips, and groin. At one point I felt my right hip and leg being pulled down as if trying to re-align it. On two occasions I felt a cold tingling moving down my back, my arms and down both legs. At the end of the healing I felt an expansion of energy in my head. My lower back feels a lot better, many thanks to you and the Psychic Surgeons for all the healing and for the help you are giving us through these times."

* "Today has been the most POSITIVE and UPLIFING of days in a very long time! I am so very grateful, to have had this healing today. Absolutely stunned at my feeling of complete wellness and have worked in the garden all day without fatigue in this heat which I would usually struggle with."

* "I had something going on with my stomach a strong pull and lots of colours, with touching on my face but, the energy was great, feeling a lot better with my anxiety not so anxious."

* "It is no exaggeration to say that Paula and the Surgeons have saved my dancing career. After struggling with a difficult and lengthy injury to my foot, I thought I would have to stop dancing completely. I was in constant pain and carrying a lot of swelling at the site of my injury. I was depressed, paranoid and having panic attacks, I was unable to rationally deal with any small problem that occurred in any area of my life.

A good friend of mine spoke to me about Paula and her work with the Surgeons and I've never looked back. Distant healing sessions with Paula every two weeks has taken away swelling and pain and cleared any anxiety associated with my injury and beyond. I went from struggling to put a shoe on my foot, to dancing on some of the world's biggest stages again. I will always be grateful to Paula and the Surgeons for keeping me in their care.

You have given me my life back."

Mr E. Watson

16. Vibrations of Nature®

Five years ago in 2015, I received a message from the Psychic Surgeons where they outlined in great detail a new future path for me to follow. I have to say the content of this message shocked me, for what they were planning was beyond any ambition I had of my own and beyond any knowledge or experience I had to bring this suggested new path to fruition.

I was already juggling many projects, as my talks and demonstrations were more in demand and my School of Psychic Surgery was about to be launched, I was running six different clinics and attending many Mind, Body Spirit events at weekends. How on earth was I going to fit this new request into my life too? I was already doing what I loved and this new path, well, it just didn't sit right with me, so I ignored it. Yes, I put it to the back of my mind. I can imagine you're thinking, what a fool, and yes, you could be right. How dare I ignore the help and guidance from the wonderful Psychic Surgeons. But did you know, Spirit are prepared to wait? They will wait and wait and when the time is right that's when their 'nudges' will begin...again.

Synchronicities began to appear in my daily life, articles in magazines, tv advertisements that caught my eye and then a friend's recommendation. Suddenly my own memory was jolted back to the time five years previously when I had received the message from the Psychic Surgeons about my potential new and exciting path.

The final synchronicity came when I had a clairvoyant reading from a lady in June of 2020 when I felt I needed to ask for guidance especially having just emerged from the first lockdown. What was I to do? In what direction should I proceed? The lady immediately linked to one of the Psychic Surgeons from the Team who was a medicine man and healer.

Who himself used berries, flowers, herbs, and bark for his healing potions. He came forward to give me a message. It was the very same message I had received from the Psychic Surgeons five years before! Those words were so familiar to me. I started to remember the message I had received from the Psychic Surgeons and inside I started to laugh, they never forget, and they had waited patiently and now was the right time to remind me of their message again and that they had a plan.

Well, this time I sat up and listened. Almost word for word the same message came through loud and clear.

"Our beloved Paula, you are going to create your own Product Range. Taking sacred oils of the earth that contain the 'Vibrations of Nature®'. Made of bark, berries, and flowers you need to market a concoction of ointments. Nature's elements add a higher vibration, and this will help the patients and it will also contain the healing energy from us, the Psychic Surgeons."

I couldn't believe it the Psychic Surgeons were creating the opportunity again but this time it was for me to take action. More information was given in this second message, I could be in no doubt what they wanted me to do, it really was as clear as day and now was the right time!

As a point of interest I researched why a person's vibration was so important. I started reading about frequencies and megahertz (MHz) something I had not studied before but as I researched more into this, I realised why the Psychic Surgeons kept mentioning to me about the importance of 'vibration'. How, during a healing session the Psychic Surgeons were increasing the patient's vibration.

It transpires that every person's body has an optimal frequency to function, and a healthy body resonates at a frequency of between 60-72 MHz

But should this frequency fall to below 58 MHz that is when disease sets in. Every illness or disease has a low vibration that influences and impacts on the functioning of the body and on the energy field surrounding it, hindering the body's ability to heal itself, and that is why the vibrational frequency needs to be raised.

There are Psychic Surgeons within the Team who are especially brought forward during a healing session, to specifically raise the vibrational energy around any disease and raise the vibrational frequency of the patient for **optimum healing.** Trapped emotions in the body's organs, muscles and tissue have a negative influence on a person's wellbeing and these trapped emotions need to be released by the Psychic Surgeons during a healing session to allow the frequency to be raised.

Now I understood, the Psychic Surgeons wanted me to launch a product range based on essential oils that are known for their higher vibrational frequency and therapeutic properties and when used on a regular basis, compliment the body's ability to heal and raise its vibration using the natural bounty of nature.

Having researched this, I just sat there in awe of the Psychic Surgeons, they are so wise and so knowledgeable. They were bringing to me further understanding of what they were doing during a healing session and what it would mean if people were to use our products to raise their vibration, whilst enjoying the benefits of the product itself. If used on a regular basis they would be taking control of their own wellness with their own selfcare. Taking something ordinary and making it into something extraordinary. Truly incredible.

That night I couldn't sleep, I was so excited, I didn't want to disappoint the Psychic Surgeons again, I had to deliver this time. But where was I to start?

The very next day I started researching on the internet, the Surgeons said they wanted an ointment, and a base cream was needed, well where was I going to get those from? They had indicated that a Company would make these for me, so more research was needed for this to find someone to assist me. They asked for essential oils to be included in the blend, but these needed to be pure, natural, and free from animal testing so it was a must that I had to source a reputable Company to include these requirements.

Then, there had to be a label, a Paula Jackson label, the Psychic Surgeons had mentioned in their message to me that I needed a logo, there was just so much to think about my mind was in a whirl. I started doodling different logos on my note pad, with decorative scrolls, different colours, different images, I asked the Surgeons, "Do you like these?" *"No, keep it simple."*

I then took my initials PJ and created coloured circles around them. I was guided by the Psychic Surgeons to choose the colour green for healing and the colour silver for purification.
When I added to the logo in the words, 'The Psychic Surgeons' and I was promptly told to remove these, which I did. *"Keep it simple"* was their message. Well my new PJ logo could not be more simple.

I then approached a printing company to enhance my logo template so that I could use it on my own photographic images, letter heads and website.

I was then guided to 'protect' my new logo and product name and so I applied to the Intellectual Property office to get my Trademark registered, and that is why when you see the PJ logo and the product range name of 'Vibrations of Nature®' you will always see the ® it is my registered trademark. It felt so exciting and so real now!

Vibrations of Nature®

Getting back to my search to find a Company who would make the products for us, took up most of my time, but in addition to this we were still sending out the distant healing too. Weeks went by, I had a couple of false starts with Companies that I thought were suitable but actually were not, for one reason or another.

As far as I was aware there was no time limit for the products to be in place, so why was I putting myself under so much pressure? Well the shock reply was given to me, *"We want you to launch the new product range in October 2020"* OMG, really? I had better get a wiggle on!

I had been getting a little despondent and asked the Psychic Surgeons, "Please would you help me?" Literally the next day as I researched on the internet a name popped up, I asked the Psychic Surgeons, is this the 'one'? *"Yes it is."* So I visited their website and to my amazement they had a vast product range from which to choose. With the Psychic Surgeons in my hands together we went through the products and the Psychic Surgeons chose each and every product that is now in our Vibrations of Nature® product range. In total we have 22 products that are either balms, creams, ointments, or oils, that can be used for selfcare, skincare, general wellness, aroma and luxurious bathing, there was something for everyone! I then approached the Company and they agreed to use my PJ labels on the selected products, so it was just a case of placing my order and waiting for the delivery.

Now, as I waited for the delivery, I prepared my website. I needed to create a 'My Shop' page specifically for the products. I prepared all the product wording for my website as I was not permitted to use the Company's product descriptions, which I quite understood. I listed the ingredients and the precautions of use for any allergies or known conditions. I was excited as there were Vegan friendly products too! Then I visited the post office to establish how much the parcel postage would be so that this could be shown against the product prices. I ordered the packaging and tried to choose recycled or eco-friendly items. Only once the products arrived would I be able to take the photographs of each product. I had in my mind all sorts of 'accessories' that I could place alongside the products and the use of fresh flowers was very important to me too, flowers from nature.

The day arrived when I was informed that the products were on their way. I was so excited, had I done everything I needed to do in preparation? The delivery van turned up with three very large boxes. I couldn't wait to see what my PJ labels looked like. I opened the first large cardboard box, every single item was wrapped in bubble wrap, it was like Christmas in October.

I couldn't get the products opened quickly enough. Finally, the first product label was revealed, and it looked brilliant. Plain and simple just like the Psychic Surgeons had asked for. I was grinning like a Cheshire cat. I spent the rest of the day unpacking each item.

Who would have thought, me, Paula Jackson would have a product range? It seemed unbelievable and yet it was happening!

The following day was spent photographing each product, staging different arrangements, props, and accessories, I felt like a photographer, just call me Davina Bailey (she laughs).
The next day was spent uploading all the product photographs onto my website. After hours of uploading and keeping my fingers crossed it would all fit and go to plan, finally it was done.
There was some tinkering to do here and there, but it was done.

I asked the Psychic Surgeons do we have a specific launch date?
"Yes, 20.10.2020 at 2pm"
Gosh, that's all the 2's. So I had a weekend off before we launched the products, but of course I had a lots of things to tick off the to do list before I was confident that everything was done and in place, but that's the perfectionist Virgo in me!

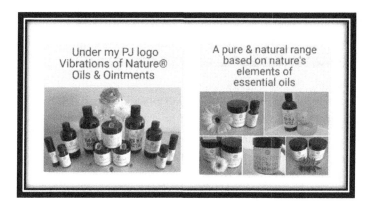

Launch day arrived, it was Tuesday 20th October 2020 and at 2pm the Psychic Surgeons asked me to launch the product range. Gosh I was nervous. I had to activate my website Shop page, send out my product launch mailshot to hundreds of people, make the announcement on all my social media sites.

Upload my newly created product video onto my You Tube channel and then send a quick note out to friends. I received messages, texts and emails congratulating me on my launch, no one knew what I had been preparing behind the scenes, but all were thrilled for me.

Almost immediately I started receiving orders! How exciting, people were responding to these wonderful products and placed their orders. I sat at my dining room table observing the COVID-19 safety precautions on handling goods, as I wrapped the orders and posted them out.

At the end of that first day I sat down and connected with the Psychic Surgeons, I told them what I had done, and that people were genuinely pleased with our product range, and I thanked them. The Psychic Surgeons now in my hands, embraced me and gave me such a squeeze, almost as if they too were saying *"Well done."*

If it had not been for the Psychic Surgeons insisting, I certainly would not have launched this luxurious range of products infused with the healing energy from the Psychic Surgeons. It really is unbelievable! The Surgeons have commented *"She's branching out!"* And that I am.

To view my full range of products, the descriptions and affordable prices please go to my website: www.paulajackson.co.uk and just click on MY SHOP page. Please note: UK deliveries only.

PRODUCT TESTIMONIALS

Dear Paula
"Well, your amazing products have really helped us since we ordered them last. Thank you to you and the Psychic Surgeons Team. My husband has found the OST ointment amazing!
His shoulder pain is now manageable - so much so that he has asked me to order some more, so he doesn't run out over Christmas! How is that for positive results, it's amazing! Thank you once again for such wonderful healing products."
C. Armiger, Wales

Dear Paula
"I'm mainly using the ointment on my hands and fingers. They're a little bit 'arthritic-ee' – stiff not painful, just knobbly joints. I really like the ointment scent. It's definitely improving the circulation to my fingers too. The knuckle joints can be a bit 'clicky' when I flex my fist, and the left hand has improved after using the ointment."
Ms. L. Johnstone

"Wow Paula what a stunning product range! The Funky Feet foot balm is beautiful, I quite literally noticed a huge improvement overnight. Nice soft feet so easily achieved.
However, the Lavender Hug in a Bottle is my favourite. Fabulous bubbles, gorgeous smell that results in a truly relaxing bath. I was very emotional and thirsty. After drinking lots of water and some help from your wonderful Restful Sleep cream I slept like a baby, after years of disruptive sleep. In the morning I felt energised, calm and well rested. These products of yours are a permanent feature in my life now! I cannot recommend Paula's products enough –
Not only are they a luxury product but a healing one too!"
Mrs DB Hampshire

"The ointments and bubble bath are great. I really feel the difference after using them."
Nicky S.

"I love the name too of 'Hug in a bottle' – what so many need right now."
Ms. HW Wales

"I was amazed at your Hug in a Bottle. It felt wonderful just like the gentle touch from the Psychic Surgeons. I've had 3 bubble baths so far using the Hug in a bottle and I feel fantastic! So happy I could burst! I can't explain it. Highly recommended."

"OST Ointment - Having only applied this to my hands twice I can feedback that I am in no pain and my hands feel so soft. This product is brilliant!"
June

"This range is lovely! OST ointment ordered and thank you, for the ointment Paula, I have been using it for 3 days now and I believe it's making a difference! I have less painful finger joints and maybe even better mobility. I'm so glad you've done this."
Helen

"I received my package today as a Christmas treat. I had a little peek, and the packaging is lovely and the stickers and thank you tags are a lovely touch. Can't wait to use them!"

"What a delight to unwrap this eczema ointment from Paula Jackson. A beautifully wrapped ointment made with love. Look Paula up for your aromatherapy gifts on her website":
www.paulajackson.co.uk

"Thank you it's such a wonderful product range to help people, especially in these difficult times."
Debbie Rowe

"Made with only the purest ingredients from nature increasing your body's vibration to allow it to rebalance and heal itself."

"To help at any stressful time the Psychic Surgeons have chosen each of these products to help relieve any stress leading to aches and pains you may be feeling."

"This range has been designed to help people outside of my healing, to raise a person's vibration to bring them back into balance to maintain or improve their wellness through selfcare."

"I'm so looking forward to helping people with their wellbeing through these higher vibrational products."

"The Psychic Surgeons are so clever, they have devised a way to continue their healing through our new product range, Oils & Ointments. There are many ailments that can be helped by using this pure and natural range, please make a visit to my website and click on MY SHOP page to view the full range, thank you."
Paula Jackson.

17. Online Learning

The Psychic Surgeons have guided me that in the future we will be creating some new online learning courses. The details of these will be found in the coming months on my School website:

www.paulajacksonschoolofpsychicsurgery.co.uk

This new strategy is of course due to the pandemic and the social distancing that hinders us from holding in person training courses. This unfortunately means the Psychic Surgeons training course is on hold for some time yet.

I will be updating the website just as soon as we are ready with our brand new Online Learning courses and I look forward to connecting with you soon.

216

18. My Poetry

Years ago when I worked in the office as a Secretary, from time to time we would have collections and cards passed around for people celebrating birthdays, or a birth, get well or leaving cards. For my written contribution I always seemed to be able to put together a little verse for that person in the form of a poem or rhyme. I have continued to write my poetry since those office days and have included some here.

The office Christmas answerphone message

(Sing this to the carol: Away in a Manger)

Hello this is Milupa we're sorry we're not here

May we wish you a Merry Christmas and a happy new year

Please leave us your message we'll get back to you soon

The 29th of December is when we resume

Now do not despair or hang up the phone

You know we can help you, please speak after the tone!

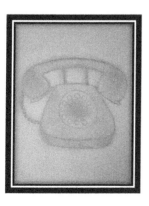

Oh Baby!

The 2nd of September was my due date
It's so warm and cosy I'm gonna be late!
Two weeks later now is the right time
To enter the world and all will be fine

But 24 hours in labour is tough
I'm feeling exhausted I've just had enough
With one last kick the show is over
I'm a baby girl with parents in clover!

So now they need to give me a name
They can't decide so make it a game
Four names in a hat I'm a lucky dip
All that effort on a no name trip!

There's Stella or Helen or Paula or Jean
Famous names from the big silver screen
The name is picked what will they call her?
Welcome into the world our daughter Paula

My dear friend Bill

Without you we feel the winter chill, my dear friend Bill
We sent you healing every day when you became so ill
The little plants you tended still sit on your windowsill
The garden is an empty space without my dear friend Bill

And still we miss your smiling face your laughter and goodwill
Especially at this Yule tide time my dear friend Bill
Our lives were so much richer for a man who had the skill
To make us laugh and feel at ease my dear friend Bill
It really was a pleasure it really was a thrill
To say he was a friend of mine my dear friend Bill

Happy 50th birthday!

You were just a slip of a girl
The day we met at Windmill Hill
At your twenty first we had a ball
A big red book as I recall

Then a fancy-dress party as you turned forty
As I remember quite drunk and naughty!
But keeping fit has been your fun
As you complete another charity run

And now you're 50 and to celebrate
We're off to Bath with all your mates
That's you and me and her and him
Out for a meal and a birthday gin!

So congratulations to you my dear friend
You're 50 years old, good wishes I send
Your youthful looks belie your years
And reading this are there some tears?

A dear and wise friend you have been to me
I bet you didn't know I could write poetry!
But this little rhyme was written for you
To say happy birthday and love to you too xx

At the theatre

And here I stand in front of you all
My dance complete I feel 10 feet tall
I am elated, I am relieved
I held my own because I believed

I kept the pace
I took my time
My energy flowed
It felt sublime

I knew the dance
I knew the score
I gave it my all
Couldn't give anymore

The curtain fell I could hear your call
Your applause, your cheers just said it all
I felt your love and I've missed that
My name is Jack and ... I am back!

Vibrations of Nature®

I introduce my latest venture
My product range, Vibrations of Nature®
Essential oil based it gives me such pleasure
To share with you, natures pure healing treasure

Oils and ointments and balms and creams
Restful sleep encouraging dreams
Sharing with you their natural combination
To assist many ailments by raising your vibration

Encouraged by the Surgeons to pursue this new range
Selling my own products feels very strange
From my PJ label, Oils and Ointments were created
And the feedback received it's very highly rated!

This product range, increases your vibration
To help the body heal of most any abrasion
The products are available at an affordable fee
Don't just take my word, please try them and see

There are twenty-two products of bottles or tubs
To pamper, to soothe, to apply with a rub
There's such a selection I don't wish to confuse
The choice is yours which ones you use

So as time goes by more people will be seeing
The therapeutic benefits for their wellbeing
It took me a while to embrace this new line
But the Surgeons were right, that now is the right time!

Celebrating 10 years!

As I recall these last ten years
Full of surprises and testing my fears
Taking me out of my comfort zone
Changing career and working from home

Helping so many with the Psychic Surgeons healing
Whether hands on, or distant, oh boy what a feeling
To know so many will return to their wellbeing
Something I never thought I would be seeing!

Learning about ailments and energy vibrations
Seeing patient's reactions as they feel the sensations
Talks and demonstrations I was so scared to do
A room full of faces waiting to hear my reviews

Two books I have written, Spirit urged me to do
To share all my knowledge and inspire you too
For without their guidance you would not see
The Psychic Surgeons faces who now work through me!

Many journey's I've made across to strange lands
Origins of the Surgeons who now work through my hands
Far flung places I never thought I would see
And a list of those yet to be visited by me

The Psychic Surgeons still have more in store
For me to bring forward and for me to explore
Being creative is something I really adore
So watch this space because there's so much more!

I can't believe ten years have gone by
It seems to have happened in the blink of an eye
I am so blessed to be in this position
So here's to the future to continue our mission.

My hope is that having read this, my 2nd book, you feel inspired and enlightened to follow your own path however it takes form. That through reading my incredible experiences with the Psychic Surgeons, who are 'The Light in my Life' it helps your understanding of Spirit and how they work and that they are here to help and guide us all.

I have shared with you in both of my books, Journal of a Psychic Surgeon and now this publication, how rewarding working with Spirit can be, and how I have embraced their connection. I have overcome some considerable changes in my life and Spirit have helped and guided me through this because I trust them.

I understand there is much more in store for me, and I embrace these changes with excitement as I know this is our mission. To know that through the amazing healing from the Psychic Surgeons we are helping so many people return to wellness, just fills my heart with joy.

Thank you so much.
Paula Jackson

19. Acknowledgements

I would like to acknowledge and thank the following people for their contribution and images used in this book.

Photo/name permission: Family Estate of Sir Arthur Conan Doyle
Psychic Art: Anna Trew, Patrick Gamble, Catherine Peiro, Museum of Miracles, France, Barbara Hudson, Paula Jackson, Fiona Frank, Lee-Anne Higgs, Gillian Berridge.
Poems: Chrissy Greenslade, Paula Jackson
Photo credit: Sea Trek, Mexico
Photography by Paula Jackson
Reference to: Singer Gerry Rafferty – Baker Street (song)
Reference to: Sir David Attenborough – BBC1 A Perfect Planet
Debbie, with thanks to my dear friend and proof reader.

20. About the Author

Having worked as a Psychic Surgeon healer and channel for the last ten years with the Spirit Psychic Surgeons I can honestly say that it has been an honour.

I completed writing this my second book at the beginning of 2021. It gave me great pleasure recalling all that has happened to me over the last three and a half years since writing my first book, 'Journal of a Psychic Surgeon' (Available through Amazon). To be able to channel for Spirit has been a delight not only for the Psychic Surgeons but connecting to other eminent spirit guides who offer their expertise and guidance. It is my hope to continue to spread the word of the wonderful Psychic Surgeons healing that is being carried out by the Psychic Surgeons.

For more information please visit Paula's website at: www.paulajackson.co.uk
where more details can be found including:

* About Paula and the Psychic Surgeons healing
* Testimonials
* The Psychic Surgeons
* Her books
* Her wellbeing product range, Vibrations of Nature®
* Or booking an appointment for the Psychic Surgeons healing

A small observation, the number of pages in this book are 227.
2+2+7=11

Made in United States
North Haven, CT
07 August 2022

22393095R00124